Peg Looms & Weaving Sticks

COMPLETE HOW-TO GUIDE AND 30+ PROJECTS

Noreen Crone-Findlay

STACKPOLE
BOOKS

Guilford, Connecticut

*To my Beloved, my best friend and husband, Jim Findlay, and also to our wonderful
family—Chloe, Clancy, James, Angus, and Alli—with gratitude and love to infinity and beyond.
And to my sister, Lesley-Ann, who is a treasure beyond measure. Also to my wonderful weaving friends:
You inspire and delight me, and I hope that this book will, in turn, inspire and delight you!
May it be a stepping stone to your creativity. Happy weaving!*

Published by Stackpole Books
An imprint of Globe Pequot
Trade Division of The Rowman & Littlefield Publishing Group, Inc.
4501 Forbes Boulevard, Suite 200, Lanham, Maryland 20706

Distributed by NATIONAL BOOK NETWORK
800-462-6420

Copyright © 2017 Rowman & Littlefield

Photography by Noreen Crone-Findlay

British Library Cataloguing in Publication Information available
Library of Congress Cataloging-in-Publication Data

Names: Crone-Findlay, Noreen, author.
Title: Peg looms and weaving sticks : complete how-to guide and 30+ projects
  / Noreen Crone-Findlay.
Description: Lanham : Stackpole Books, an imprint of Globe Pequot, Trade
  Division of The Rowman & Littlefield Publishing Group, Inc., [2017]
Identifiers: LCCN 2017018886 (print) | LCCN 2017019646 (ebook) | ISBN
  9780811764810 (e-book) | ISBN 9780811716123 (pbk. : alk. paper)
Subjects: LCSH: Hand weaving--Patterns.
Classification: LCC TT848 (ebook) | LCC TT848 .C6845 2017 (print) | DDC
  746.1/4041--dc23
LC record available at https://lccn.loc.gov/2017018886

♾™ The paper used in this publication meets the minimum requirements of American National Standard for Information Sciences—Permanence of Paper for Printed Library Materials, ANSI/NISO Z39.48-1992.

First Edition

Printed in the United States of America

Contents

Acknowledgments

Without peg looms and weaving sticks upon which to work, this book couldn't happen, and so I am most grateful to the generosity of the following lovely people: Donna and Gary McFarland from Dewberry Ridge, dewberryridge.com; Lynette Richter from Daisy Hill Handiworks, daisyhillhandiworks.blogspot.com; Dennis Riley from Daegrad Tools, daegrad.co.uk; Jules Kliot at Lacis Museum of Lace & Textiles, lacis.com.

A weaving book also does not happen without yarn, so I am hugely grateful to my main yarn supplier: Thank you, John Little at briggsandlittle.com. Thank yous also go to the gracious people at Lion Brand. My daughter-in-love/law, Alliston Findlay, of nomadfibreworks.com, is a master spinner and I appreciate how she blesses me with her beautiful hand-spun yarns.

I am so grateful to all the people who have worked so hard to bring this book into being, beginning with editor Deb Smith, who began the process at Stackpole Books, and Candi Derr and Julie Marsh, who took the book to completion at Rowman & Littlefield. Thanks also to the production team, especially Wendy Reynolds. I am very grateful to you! Thank you!

Introduction

I first began weaving with peg looms and weaving sticks almost two decades ago, and I am still madly in love with them. In fact, the more I work with them, the more I love them. I am constantly astonished and delighted by the creative potential of these simple little looms.

I have absolutely loved developing new ways of working with peg looms and weaving sticks. My hope is that the projects and techniques in this book will be a source of inspiration for you, stepping stones that will enhance and expand your delight in peg loom weaving. I am looking forward to seeing what you weave based on these designs and techniques.

This book was written with a sense of joy and completely comes from a place of love. I hope that you will feel that in its pages and come up with your own creative projects and designs.

This, my friends, is my wish for you. Happy weaving!

With love and gratitude,
Noreen

Getting to Know Your Peg Loom

Before we begin, I am going to go pour myself a cup of tea, and I suggest that you pour one for yourself—or whatever you like to linger over while chatting with a friend. You see, this chapter is very much a conversation. As I am writing it, I am remembering the questions that people have asked me in workshops, on Facebook, and on Ravelry, and I am going to answer them for you to the best of my ability. Even though I have been weaving with peg looms and weaving sticks for decades now, these are my opinions, based on my experiences, so my answers might not quite fit your circumstances. So I'd like you to take my opinions and use them to form your own answers.

Let's pour our tea, and get started.

What Is a Peg Loom?

A little bit of confusion swirls around the exact nature of a peg loom. Some looms on the market are called "peg looms," but they are not the kind of peg loom that we are going to be working with in this book.

Those "other peg looms" are quite different from ours. They are frame looms that use nails or plastic or wooden pegs to hold the warp strands strung in tension back and forth starting from the upper to the lower edges of the loom. The weft goes under and over the warp strands until the loom is full.

The peg looms in this book could probably be more accurately described as "dowel looms." Dowels, called "pegs," fit into holes drilled into the base so they stand vertically and firmly in place. If the pegs don't stand firmly in place, they will fall out and pull together while you're weaving and the tension will be awful. Test the pegs to make sure they are firmly in place before you buy a peg loom. If you can't test the loom yourself (perhaps because

you are buying it online), be sure to buy from a trusted, reputable loom builder.

Just slightly above the base, each peg has a hole drilled in it so warp strands can pass through the peg and hang freely behind the base. The weaving is done on the pegs. When the pegs are full, they are gently lifted out of the base, then eased up through the weaving until the weaving is resting on the warp strands and the pegs are empty, ready to be filled with weaving again.

In this way, our peg looms work very differently from the other peg looms. Think of the dowel pegs as lengths of warp strand that froze in place—they no longer need to be held in tension the way string warp strands do. And, because the top ends of the frozen warp strands (aka the pegs) don't need to be tied to the upper side of a loom, voila, there is no upper side to our peg loom!

The weft (the yarn that does the filling up of the weaving) ambles around the pegs on its path to becoming a finished piece. In reality, the weft yarn is still going over/under and under/over the warp strands. But when you are weaving on the peg loom, what you see is weft going behind or passing in front of the peg.

Peg looms have another great advantage: The finished length of the weaving is not determined by the size of the peg loom, only by the length of the warp strands chosen for the weaving. Peg looms and weaving sticks can also be easily used to create all kinds of free-form shapes using short row techniques. But we'll chat more about that later.

Another kind of peg loom, but not the kind we are working with in this book.

The type of peg loom we will be using in this book.

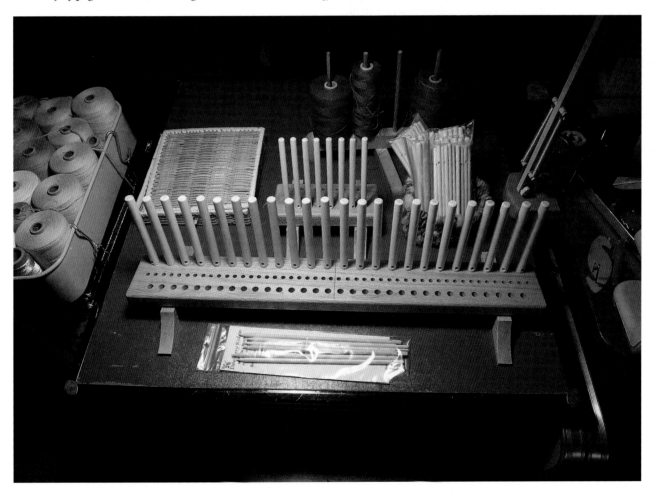

Weaving stick.

What Are Weaving Sticks?

Weaving sticks are dowels or rods with one flattened end and one gently pointed end. Near the flattened end, a hole is drilled through the dowel.

Weaving sticks are meant to be held in your hand while you weave, so they are most often sold in sets of four or six. They don't usually fit into a base, but some companies make different versions that have a large clothespin or small wooden base. Weaving sticks have a more streamlined end than pegs, and the hole is closer to the end. Weaving sticks are wonderfully portable, and you can do an amazing amount of very satisfying weaving with them.

Can you use the pegs from a peg loom as weaving sticks? Yes, in a pinch, but the shaping of the end of weaving sticks and the placement of the hole closer to the end make weaving sticks more efficient for hand holding than the pegs from your loom.

Because weaving sticks are held together in your hand, with no spaces between them, they yield a denser and firmer finished fabric than a peg loom. This can be a great advantage in some projects.

How Do I Choose a Loom?

If you are trying to decide which set of weaving sticks or which loom to buy, think about the projects you want to make in the context of the following questions and consider my opinions. Remember, these truly are my opinions. Yes, I have put decades of work into weaving with peg looms and weaving sticks, but not everyone weaves the same or has the same experiences. So if these "answers" don't work for you, that's just fine. As you gain more experience, you will find the perfect loom or

A variety of peg looms and weaving sticks are available in different sizes.

weaving sticks that you will love to pieces. Trust me on this one: The more I weave on peg looms and with weaving sticks, the more I adore them! I know you will, too.

What is your favorite weight of yarn to work with?

Answer A: Very fine yarns and threads

Choose pegs or weaving sticks that are ⅛" (3 mm), ³⁄₃₂" (2.4 mm), or ¼" (6 mm) in diameter.

Answer B: Medium weight yarns, light weight roving, narrow strips of T-shirt yarn

Choose pegs or weaving sticks that are ¼" (6 mm) or ⅜" (9 mm) in diameter.

Answer C: Heavy weight yarns, thick fabric strips, bulky yarns held together

Choose pegs or weaving sticks that are ⅜" (9 mm) or ½" (1.3 cm) in diameter.

Does the spacing of the holes on a peg loom make a difference?

Yes! The more space there is between the holes, the more weft you are going to need to fill those gaps; otherwise, you run the risk of ending up with flimsy, gappy, unhappy fabric. So, if you have wide spaces, choose thicker weft and lots more rows to give a pleasing fabric that is worth the time, effort, and cost of materials.

Ideally, you should choose a loom that has proportionally spaced pegs, which means that the space between the pegs is no wider than the diameter of the pegs.

What's the best height for pegs?

If you plan on doing a lot of color changing and patterning work or if you plan on using templates (more on that later, too), then definitely choose longer pegs. They should be at least 6" (15 cm) tall measured from the base of the loom to the tip of the peg. If you don't plan to do pattern weaving or use templates, choose shorter pegs and advance the weft more often.

What's the best length for weaving sticks?

The length of weaving sticks depends on the size of the sticks and what you plan to weave on them. For instance, 10" (25 cm) is great for projects like the Bag for a Yoga Mat or Peg Loom (see page 141), but 6" (15 cm) actually works better for the Nreenie Doll (page 91).

Should I buy more than one set of weaving sticks?

Buying more than one set of weaving sticks depends on what you want to weave. For example, the Square Baskets (see page 75) are woven with seven weaving sticks, so it's good to order two sets. But the Nreenie Dolls (see page 91) are woven with only three weaving sticks, so a set of four or six weaving sticks is just fine.

What size peg loom should I buy? Is bigger better?

Bigger isn't always better. The wider the fabric woven on a peg loom, the more challenging it is to ease it into shape after weaving. I prefer to weave panels or sections that are a maximum of about 15" (37.5 cm) wide and then stitch the panels together. See the Cozy Roving Shawl (see page 161) for instructions on connecting panels.

Should I buy a peg loom with multiple rows of pegs?

I like to have the option of weaving with different size pegs, so I love having three rows of pegs.

What other stuff do I need?

Depending on which projects you are going to make, you may need embellishments like found objects, beads, buttons, jewelry findings, charms, ribbon, lace, and roving for felting. The tools and materials you'll need for a specific project will be listed with the instructions for that piece.

Is weaving on a peg loom quick and easy?

That answer depends on the project. Some projects are really quick and easy to make; others are mind-bendingly slow and involved. Sorry, but it's true. Also, the techniques and your familiarity with them are factors; the more familiar you are with weaving, the faster the project will go. Some of the techniques I have developed may seem like head-scratchers at first, but with repetition, they do become very accessible.

Most people are surprised that the finishing process with peg loom weaving is so slow. I prefer to think of it as meditative or contemplative. But that doesn't keep me from whining at times: *Oh, this is taking forever!*

Is there one specific way to set up a peg loom for weaving?

Comfort is essential when weaving. Position the loom on a table with the weaving at a comfortable height or on your lap so there is no strain on your wrists, shoulders, or tendons of the lower arms. When you are comfortable with the motion of weaving on the peg loom, you will be able to weave longer and more happily.

Find a loom setup that is comfortable for you.

CHAPTER 2

Basic Techniques

In this chapter, we'll take a look at all the basic techniques you'll need to get started. Make sure you understand each of these techniques completely and practice them thoroughly. They are the building blocks for a successful adventure in peg loom weaving, and knowing them well will make your path forward into more advanced projects much easier.

Start with Warp Strands

Warp strands are the strands of yarn that form the vertical framework of the weaving. They are passed through the holes in the pegs and hang freely from the back of the loom.

Equipment

- scissors
- tape measure
- peg loom
- warp threader
- 2 C-clamps or a tape measure or a warping board (if you have one and are used to working with it)

Choose the Warp Yarn

The warp yarn strands need to be smooth and very strong so the weft can slide down them easily without catching or breaking. Very stretchy yarns are not a good choice, nor are highly textured yarns. Some people have used fabric strips successfully, but they can tear, fray, snag, and cause the weft to catch, so they are not recommended for warp.

The warp strands should be thick enough so they fill the channel formed by the weaving stick or peg fully, but not too thick, as it will be difficult to advance the weft down the warp when they are too thick or there are too many strands in the warp bundle.

The warp strands will be covered completely by the weft strands.

Determine the Working Length of the Warp Strands

Decide on the finished length of the piece and add 12" (30 cm) for the hems.

Determine the Full Length of the Warp Strands

Remember that the working length of the warp is measured from the peg to the yarn ends. The actual length of the warp strands is double the working length, as they need to be folded in half, with the peg at the center point of the warp strands.

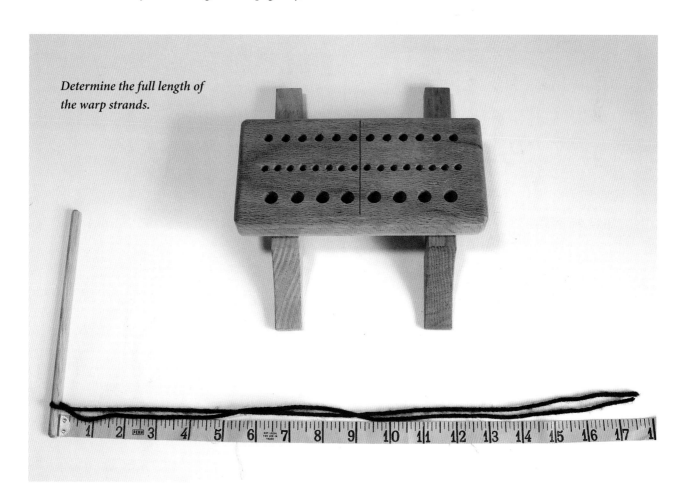

Determine the full length of the warp strands.

Measure the Warp Strands and Warp the Peg Loom

Warping the peg loom means to thread the warp into the pegs, then place the pegs into the holes of the loom. Once the warp strands are measured and cut, they are threaded into the holes, and voilà—that's it! Your loom is warped and you are ready to weave.

I use one of two ways to measure warp strands.

Method 1: C-Clamps

1. Place 2 C-clamps the desired distance apart and wrap the warp strands around them.

2. Cut the warp strands at one clamp.

3. Push the peg threader through the peg and pull the required number of strands of warp yarn held together through the hole in the peg. Bring the ends of the warp strands together and slide the peg up to the fold.

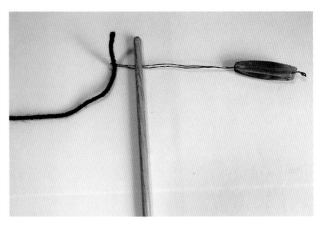

Method 2: Tape Measure

1. Push the peg threader through the peg and pull the required number of strands of warp yarn through the hole in the peg.

2. Place the peg in the loom and pinch the end of a tape measure to the end of the yarn.

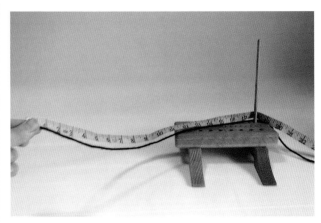

3. Pull out the required length of warp, running the warp strands along the tape measure to the desired length from the yarn end to the peg.

4. Drop the tape measure and smooth the warp strands off the balls of yarn along the measured length.

5. Snip the yarn from the balls at the desired length: the working length.

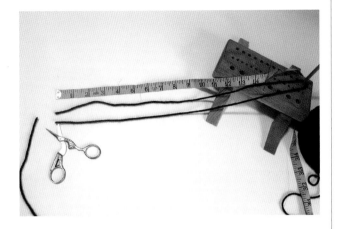

6. The fold of yarn is at the peg, and the yarn is doubled.

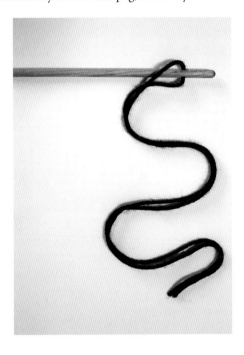

7. Repeat this process for the remaining pegs.

Knots for Weaving

HALF HITCH KNOT

The half hitch knot is used to start and end the weaving on peg looms and weaving sticks. Half hitches are also used to make decorative cords and rings.

1. Make a letter e with the weft yarn.

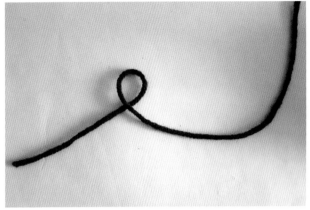

2. Slip it on to the peg or weaving stick.

PARTIAL KNOT

The partial knot is simply the first half of the square knot.

1. Place one end of the yarn over and then under the other yarn end, and pull it up.

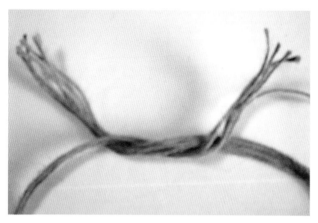

The partial knot is always secured by having the ends woven into the channel.

SQUARE KNOT

1. Left over right and under.

2. Right over left and under.

3. Pull up firmly to secure.

SURGEON'S KNOT

1. Left over right and under, repeated, so the left goes over the right and under again.

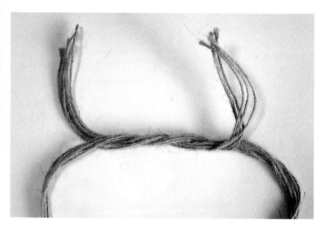

2. Right over left and under.

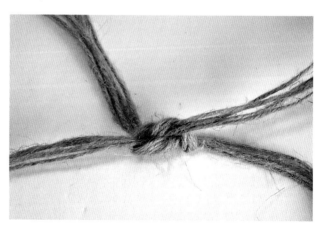

3. Pull up firmly to secure.

How to Weave on a Peg Loom

The weaving is done with yarn that is called the "weft." The weft strands are the horizontal filling of the weaving. They travel in and out across the loom, going in front of and behind the pegs to cover the pegs and then the warp strands completely.

Start the Weaving

1. Make a half hitch knot and place it on the left-hand edge peg.

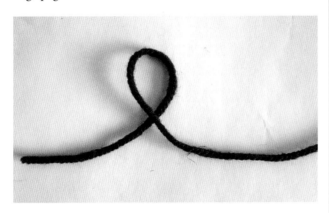

2. First pass: Bring the yarn in front of the next peg and behind the one beside it. Repeat this process across the loom. (*Note:* The yarn colors have changed from the previous photo to better illustrate the weaving.)

3. Second pass: Working from right to the left, bring the yarn around the edge peg and take it across to the left, going in front of the pegs that you went behind and behind the pegs you went in front of in the first pass.

4. These two passes complete one row, and now you are weaving on your peg loom!

Advance the Weaving on a Peg Loom

When the weaving fills the pegs, you will need to advance the weft down the warp. Here's how:

1. When the weft almost reaches the top of the pegs, it's time to advance the warp. One by one, lift the pegs out of the holes on the loom. It is usually easier to begin at the center of the loom. It's important to keep the weft yarn at the top of the pegs, so be careful as you ease each of the pegs out of their holes.

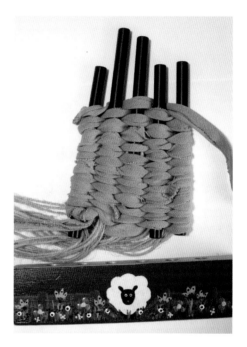

2. Place your nondominant hand on the beginning edge of the weaving and apply light pressure to the weaving to keep it from bunching up.

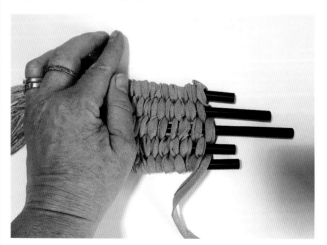

3. With your dominant hand, ease each peg up through the weaving. Stroke the weaving down the warp strands.

4. Place each peg, one by one, back into its correct hole. When returning the pegs to their holes, it's easier to begin at one edge and work across the loom. Be very careful to not cross pegs by placing them in the wrong holes, and don't skip holes.

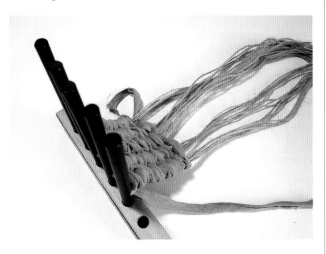

5. Carry on weaving and advancing the weaving until you are done.

Troubleshooting

Q: Do you have too many warp strands threaded into the pegs or weaving sticks?

A: Try pulling one out to see if the warp moves more freely through the channel.

Q: Is the weft too snaggy? Try one of these solutions:

- Weave the weft slightly looser, decreasing the tension on the pegs or weaving sticks.

- Advance the weft more frequently.

- Pack the weft more loosely on the pegs or weaving sticks.

After the Weaving Is Complete

When you have completed the weaving, straighten out the warp strands and undo any tangles.

1. Lift the pegs out of the holes. Pull the pegs up through the weaving so there are warp ends at both ends. The weaving often bunches up, so it needs to be eased out to its full length.

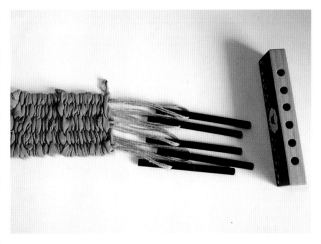

2. Starting from the beginning of the weaving, place one hand on the weaving to hold it in place. With the other hand, using a light touch, scoot a few inches of weaving along the warp. This will create gaps along the warp that you will fill as you move the weft strands.

3. Continue to move the weft down the warp strands until it is evenly distributed to the final dimensions of the piece.

4. Finish the edges of the weaving to lock in the warp strands, using one of the edge finishes (see page 17). It is acceptable to use a different finish for the lower edge than the upper edge, depending on the piece.

Tip If the weaving starts to snag and pull up, check for "gossiping" warp strands. These warp strands sneak into a neighboring channel instead of minding their own business. Release the sneaky warp strands by tweaking them out of the wrong channel and flicking the weaving slightly.

How to Weave with Weaving Sticks

Working with weaving sticks is similar to working with the pegs on the peg loom. Follow these steps to get started.

Measure the Warp Strands and Warp the Weaving Sticks

1. Determine the length of the working warp strands. (Remember that the working length is the length of the finished weaving plus 12" [30 cm].) The cut length of the warp strands will need to be twice as long as the working length so they can be folded in half to create the working length. Decide how many strands of yarn will be used for the warp strands.

2. Thread the warp strands through the holes in the weaving sticks using a peg threader, a floss threader from the pharmacy, or nylon Flexi-needles from the fabric shop. If you can't find a floss threader, fold a short length of wire in half and put a bead on the end; then, twist the ends to secure the bead.

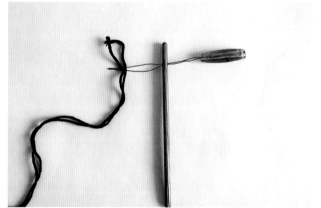

3. Push the threader through the hole and take the yarn through it. Pull the threader back through the hole to pull the yarn ends through the weaving stick.

4. Bring the warp ends up even, giving them a slight tug to ensure that the warp strands are smooth and centered in the weaving stick.

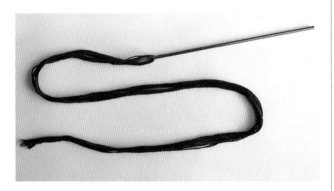

Start the Weaving

1. Start with a half hitch knot. Make an e shape with the yarn, leaving a couple of inches at the end. Place the e on the weaving stick at one edge.

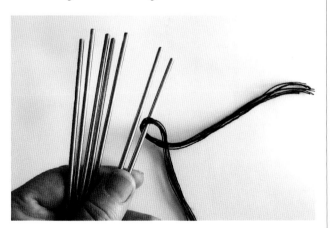

2. Hold the weaving sticks slightly fanned out in one hand. Weave the yarn in front and behind, across the sticks to the other side.

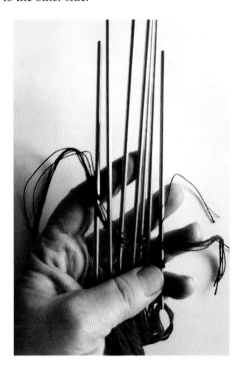

3. Weave the yarn back to the starting point, going behind the weaving sticks that you wove in front of last time and in front of the ones that you went behind. Remember: One row of weaving equals one full pass to the left and one full pass back to the right, so that every weaving stick has weft in front of and behind it.

Tip For the desired length, keep the tension light and don't pull in too tightly.

Advance the Warp

1. When the weaving fills the weaving sticks, ease the center weaving sticks up a little, then the edge sticks.

2. As the weaving grows, slide the weaving sticks up through the weaving, which will move the weaving down the warp strands. Place the weaving on the table or against your leg and smooth it along the warp strands. Hold the warp strands with your nondominant hand and stroke the weaving with your dominant hand.

Tip The weaving can bunch up, so be sure to distribute the weft along the warp strands so they are not solid like a board. The exception to this statement is when weaving a handle. Then, the weaving should be extra dense and firm. It will last longer and be more satisfying than a flimsy, too loosely woven band.

3. Advance the weaving down the warp strands until there are about 3 or 4" (7.5 to 10 cm) of warp strands at the end. If you are leaving a fringe and want it longer, then allow for it when measuring and cutting the warp strands. Leave the same length of warp strands unwoven at the top of the band.

End the Weaving

1. Make a half hitch knot around the last weaving stick. Make an e shape with the yarn over your index finger. Slip the e onto the peg. Pull it up firmly. Snip the warp strands from the weaving sticks at the fold.

Finishing Techniques

The weft in peg loom and weaving sticks weaving has a tendency to bunch up, so the first step in finishing your weaving is to distribute the weft strands along the warp strands to the required dimensions of the finished piece. On larger pieces, this can take some time, so be prepared to do some smoothing, nudging, and redirecting of the weft strands along the warp strands.

The finishing work done on your weaving is the secret to a successful and satisfying completed project. Warp ends have to be secured by some form of knotting, and all weft and warp ends have to be woven in.

The way you tie off the warp ends of your weaving will vary depending on the project. Finishing flat pieces that have a beginning and ending edge is different from finishing round or shaped pieces in which the warp ends are tied together.

Finishing techniques can feel slow and frustrating if you are not expecting to have to spend some time on them. If you think of the finishing as a contemplative and meditative quiet time, then it's actually quite pleasant. It's another chance to enjoy the yarns and delight in the weaving that you have done.

Warp End Finishes

To keep the warp strands from accidentally being pulled out of the finished weaving, it is essential to lock them in. There are many ways of doing this, mostly by knotting the ends in various ways.

DOUBLE DAMASCUS EDGING

The double Damascus edge, made of Damascus knots, is the best choice for finishing edges that will have fringe or for warp ends that are going to be woven in later.

1. Cut the pegs from the warp strands.

2. Smooth the warp strands out on a table with the strands at the edge.

3. Begin at the right-hand side: Divide the first set of warp strands in half. Take the right-hand strands over the left-hand strands, behind, and up through the loop. This forms the first Damascus knot.

4. Pull up gently, snugging the Damascus knot against the fell line of the weaving (the edge of the weaving that has just been woven). Lay the working set of strands at the top on the weaving.

5. Divide the next set of warp strands in half. Take the set of strands on which the previous Damascus knot was tied over half of the next set of strands. Use this set of strands to work the next Damascus knot. Lay the strands on the weaving.

6. Repeat until all strands are knotted. Tie the last two sets of strands a second time to secure them.

7. Flip the warp strands down, and work another row of Damascus knots across the piece.

For a video on how to work the Damascus Edge, please see: https://youtu.be/bRkvE0Y3O9c.

OVERHAND KNOTS

1. Divide the warp strands so that half come from one channel and half come from the adjacent channel.

2. Wrap the warp strands around a latch hook, take the ends into the mouth of the hook, and pull them through the wrap.

SIMPLE FRINGE

After securing the warp strands with double Damascus knots or overhand knots, trim the warp ends and leave them as a warp strand fringe. This warp strand finish is the least durable finish and should be used judiciously, if at all.

TWISTED FRINGE

A warp-twisting device twists clusters of warp strands around each other. Knots are then tied at the ends to form a more enduring fringe. It is essential to take half the strands from one channel and half from the next to form a secure twisted fringe.

WOVEN-IN WARP STRANDS

Woven-in warp strands give a clean, elegant finished edge. The warp ends can be woven in a with a blunt darning, craft, or tapestry needle or with a latch hook. Crochet hooks are not recommended as they can snag the weft strands from inside.

Weaving in Warp Ends with a Tapestry Needle

1. Thread one set of warp ends into the needle.

2. Take the needle into the appropriate channel.

3. Bring the needle out when it has gone as far as possible, pull up, and then re-enter the channel, carrying the warp end along the inside of the channel. Trim any little tufts at the ends.

Weaving in Warp Ends with a Latch Hook

1. Insert a latch hook into the channel a couple of inches away from the knot. Bring the hook out at the knot.

2. Open the latch and place the ends in the hook. Pull the hook back through the channel.

3. Insert the hook again, bring it out at the ends, and repeat the pulling process. Trim any little tufts at the ends.

MACHINE-STITCHED ANCHORING

The only project in this book that has machine stitching along the hem is the Upholstered Chair (see page 151). Because of the stresses upholstery fabric has to tolerate, the edge must be extra secure. Work the Damascus edge first, then machine stitch, and finish by weaving the warp ends inside the channels of weaving.

TIED ROD, DOWEL, OR BRANCH

1. Fold the warp strands up and onto the weaving. Lay a dowel, rod, or branch just above it.

2. Beginning at the center of the weaving, take one set of warp strands up and over the rod.

3. Bring the warp strands behind the rod and then back in front of the rod.

4. Tie the first half of the surgeon's knot (over and under and through the loop twice) over the warp strands at the fell line (the edge of the weaving).

5. Pull up on the ends to gently snug the rod, dowel, or branch against the weaving.

6. Work from one side of the center, then the other side of the center, all the way to the edges.

7. Adjust any unevenness by tightening up the ends.

8. Tie the second half of the knot (over and under and through the loop once) on all the strands across the weaving.

9. After both ends of the weaving are finished, weave in all ends.

WARP END TASSEL

Leave extra weft at the beginning and end of the weaving when doing a tassel finish.

1. Gather the warp ends together to form the tassel.

2. Wrap the weft ends around a cluster of warp ends, pulling the weaving into a soft curve at the edge.

3. Lay a tapestry needle or small-gauge latch hook over the warp ends with the eye of the needle or the hook facing toward the warp ends.

4. Wrap the warp ends and needle or hook several times with the weft strands, pulling up fairly tightly.

5. Thread the weft ends into the eye of the needle or place them into the crook of the hook.

6. Pull through the wraps.

7. Insert the hook or needle through the wraps and pull the weft ends through the wrap one more time.

8. Thread the needle or hook through the center channel of weaving and pull the weft ends inside to secure.

9. Slightly down from the weft wraps, wrap the tassel with a strand of yarn (you can use the same color as the warp strands or a contrasting color) two times and pull up firmly to pull in the neck of the tassel.

Tie a knot, leaving ends that are at least as long as the warp strands.

10. Take the ends through the eye of a needle or use a fine latch hook, and pull them down through the wraps.

11. Smooth all the warp ends and trim the ends of the tassel.

WARP STRAND YARN BABIES

To make the head, follow the instructions for the Warp End Tassel.

To make the arms:

1. Separate 5 to 7 warp strands on the left and right sides of the bundle for the arms and lift them out horizontally.

2. Wrap 1 strand of yarn around the arm to form the wrist. Tie a very tight knot; then, trim the ends close to the knot.

3. Trim the arms fairly close to the wrist to form the hands.

4. Repeat this process for the second arm.

> *Tip* A drop of fray-stop glue on the knots is useful if the yarns are slippery and look like they might slide off or come undone.

To make the waist:

1. Wrap 1 strand of yarn around the body to form the waist, leaving ends that are as long as the rest of the body.

2. Tie a very tight knot; then, smooth the ends down.

To make a skirt or legs:

Decide if you are making a skirt or legs. To make a skirt, trim the strands to form the hem of the skirt.

To make legs, divide the strands in half and wrap 1 strand of yarn near the bottom of one of the legs to form the ankle; tie a very tight knot, then trim the ends close to the knot. Repeat for the other leg. Trim the yarn below the knots fairly close to the ankles to form the feet.

HALF HITCH CORDS AND RINGS

When working with a single peg or weaving stick, a closely packed series of half hitch knots progresses along the warp strands to form small circles or long cords that can be used as decorative elements or edge binding. To make a cord for appliquéd motifs or the edge of a piece, measure the working length of warp strands and just keep making the half hitches until a sturdy cord is formed.

Half Hitch Cords

1. Cut the desired length of warp strands. Using 1 peg or weaving stick, thread the warp strand(s) through the hole in the peg or weaving stick.

2. Hold the peg in your nondominant hand and take the yarn over the index finger of your dominant hand, forming a loop like the letter *e*.

3. Insert the peg into the loop, lift it off your finger, then snug the yarn gently to the peg. Slide the half hitch knot along the peg or weaving stick. When the peg or weaving stick is full, slide the half hitches onto the warp strands.

4. Repeat steps 2 and 3, with the half hitch knots pushed closely together, until the cord is the desired length.

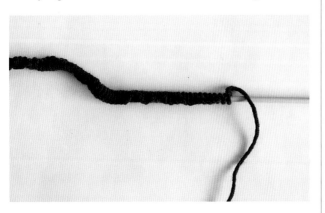

5. Ease the half hitches along the warp strands until the beginning of the cord is a few inches from the end.

Single Peg or Weaving Stick Half Hitch Ring

1. Using 1 weaving stick or peg and 1 strand of warp, make 15 half hitch knots. Ease them down the warp strands. Leave a few inches at the end, then snip the warp strands a few inches away from the half hitch knots.

2. Pull up on the warp strands and tie a tight square knot to form the ring.

3. Thread the weft end into a darning needle and stitch through the top of the adjacent knot to close the ring.

JOINED AND LOCKED

This finish is used to join the warp strands from the beginning of the weaving to the warp strands at the end of the weaving; tie them together with square knots and then weave them in. The ends in the Mobius Strip Cowl (see page 28), the side section of the Pillbox Hat (see page 41), and the ends in the Circles and Squares Rug (see page 72) are all joined and locked edges.

Steaming and Blocking

Steaming and blocking are finishing techniques that help to create the desired shape of the completed weaving.

Never push down hard on the weaving with a steam iron. Always hold the iron slightly above the weaving and pulse bursts of steam at the piece. After steaming the weaving, ease it out to the full dimensions of the template or desired finished measurements. Block it by pinning the edges to a cushion or ironing board until the weaving is completely dry.

Stitching Pieces Together

1. Place the edges of the pieces together.

2. Bring the needle up through the first stitch on one of the pieces.

3. Cross to the corresponding stitch on the other piece and take the needle through the stitch.

4. Bring the needle back across and through the edge of the other piece.

5. Repeat steps 2, 3, and 4 until the pieces are sewn together.

6. When the stitching is complete, weave in any yarn ends.

CHAPTER 3

Getting Started

These two great little projects are a fun way to get started with peg loom weaving. The first one is the Mobius Strip Cowl. You have several options to make this project uniquely yours. If you don't want it to twist, don't fold it. Just bring the ends together to create an elegant circular cowl. If you don't want a cowl, just weave yourself a scarf.

The second project is the Cozy Headband, designed to give you a chance to experiment with finishing techniques on a small scale. Try the tassel or opt for Damascus knots instead.

Either project will give you a delightful introduction to weaving with a peg loom.

Mobius Strip Cowl

A cowl is a wonderfully comfortable alternative to a scarf. Because it is a circle, it never slips off your neck and the ends don't get in the way. Flipping the weaving over once before stitching the ends together creates the mobius and shapes the cowl. Choose plain yarn for elegant simplicity or weave with self-striping or patterned yarn to make a cowl that looks deceptively complex. Patterned yarns can do all the work of changing colors for you.

Equipment

- Dewberry Ridge 15" (37.5 cm)-wide peg loom
- 14 pegs, ¼" (6 mm) in diameter
- tape measure
- scissors
- warp threader
- blunt tapestry needle
- latch hook

Yarn

- Warp: #4 medium weight acrylic yarn, 3 balls, 1.7 oz./50 g each
- Weft: Unique by Lion Brand (100% acrylic; 3.5 oz./100 g, 109 yd./100 m), #210 Circus, 1 ball

Specs

- WPI: 9 wraps per 1" (2.5 cm)
- Finished Measurements: Approximately 30" (75 cm) long by 6" (15 cm) wide

Notes

The Mobius Strip Cowl is woven with 1 strand of yarn for the weft. The warp is 3 strands of yarn held together.

WEAVING

1. The working length of the warp strands is 42" (105 cm), so the cut length of the warp strands before threading them into the pegs is 84" (210 cm). Here's the math: 30" (75 cm) long cowl + 12" (30 cm) to tie off ends = 42". Then 42" x 2 = 84".

2. Thread the warp strands into the pegs and weave 36" (90 cm).

3. Distribute the weft evenly along the warp strands, making sure there are 6" (15 cm) of warp for finishing at both ends of the weaving.

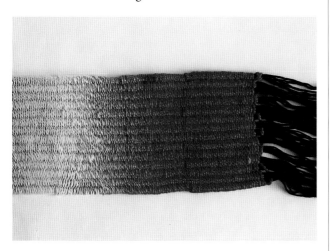

4. Fold the weaving at the center to form the twist for the mobius.

5. Bring the ends of the weaving together. Carefully line up the channels so they match.

6. Tie square knots all the way across.

FINISHING

Weave in the ends. Weave half of the warp strands to one side of the knots and the other half into the channels on the other side of the knots.

Cozy Headband

This warm and fluffy headband is embellished with a tassel made from the contrasting color of the warp. Instead of a tassel, try finishing it with a double Damascus edge and weaving in the warp strands. Any soft, comfortable, cozy yarn or roving is appropriate and will look wonderful in this quick and easy project.

Equipment

- 6 weaving sticks ⅜" (9 mm) in diameter and 10" (25 cm) long for the headband
- 2 weaving sticks ¼" (6 mm) in diameter for the button
- warp threader
- scissors
- tape measure or ruler
- felting needle (optional, to push in any ends and shape loops that may be erratic)

Yarn

- Warp: Atlantic by Briggs & Little (100% pure wool; 4 oz./113 g, 135 yd./123 m), #55 Violet, 1 ball
- Weft: Country Roving by Briggs & Little (100% pure wool; 8 oz./227 g, 85 yd./78 m), #73 Red, 1 ball

Specs

- WPI: 6 wraps per 1" (2.5 cm)
- Finished Measurements: Approximately 3½" (8.75 cm) wide by 27" (67.5 cm) long

WEAVING

1. Warp 6 weaving sticks with 3 strands of yarn held together for each stick. The working length of the warp strands is 39" (97.5 cm) long. The cut length is 78" (195 cm).

2. With 6 weaving sticks or pegs, weave 1" (2.5 cm).

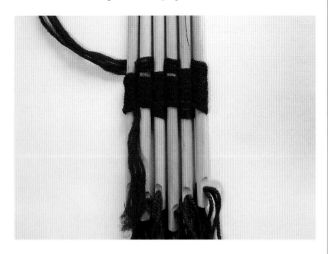

3. Buttonhole: Weave 1½" (3.75 cm) on 3 weaving sticks. Cut the weft yarn.

4. Rejoin the yarn and weave 1½" (3.75 cm) on the remaining 3 weaving sticks.

5. Weave on all weaving sticks until the headband is 27" (67.5 cm) long.

FINISHING

Advance the warp until you have about 6" (15 cm) at each end of the weaving.

1. Make a tassel (see page 22) at the buttonhole end of the headband.

2. Work a double Damascus edge (see page 17) at the other end. Weave the ends in.

3. With the Violet yarn and the ¼" (6 mm) weaving sticks, make a circle for a button (see page 52).

4. Try on the headband and determine where to stitch the button. Mark the location with a pin.

5. Place a weaving stick on the back of the button with half the warp ends on both sides of it.

6. Take the warp ends through the headband at the pin and bring them out on the wrong side, at least ½" (1.3 cm) apart.

7. Tie a very firm knot against the weaving stick.

8. Pull the weaving stick out of the knot.

9. Weave all yarn ends into the headband.

CHAPTER 4

Weaving Circles

I t may seem challenging to weave circles on a peg loom or weaving sticks, but it is actually quite easy. The secret is in weaving short rows that shape the circle like slices of pie. Weaving circles enables you to make an unlimited number of projects—everything from buttons and brooches to baskets, hats, masks, and a tour de force vest. In chapter 5, circles are combined with squares to make a unique rug.

How to Weave a Circle

The spacing of pegs varies among loom builders and even in different models of looms from the same builder. This difference in spacing will affect the final size of the woven piece, so you may need to experiment to find the perfect number of pegs to weave the size of circle you wish to make. The weight of your yarn or using roving or strips of fabric instead of yarn can also change the finished size of the circle.

FIGURE OUT THE LENGTH OF THE WARP STRANDS

1. Decide how large you want the circle to be.

2. Multiply the diameter of the circle by 3.14 and add 10" (25 cm) for the tie-off ends. The resulting number is the working length of the warp strands for the outside edge of the circle. Remember, you'll need to double this measurement to get the cut length of the warp strands because they are folded at the peg to give the working length.

To determine the length of the warp strands in the middle of a 10" (25 cm)-diameter circle, the radius would be roughly 5" (12.5 cm). So, 5 x 3.14 = 15.7". Round that up to 16" and add 6" for knotting and weaving in the ends and the working length would be 22" (55 cm). Double that number to get the cut length—44" (110 cm)—which is the length of the strip when it is doubled and folded around the peg.

Typically, the center peg only needs about 12" (30 cm) of warp strands. The rest of the warp strands for the pegs or weaving sticks can be staggered in length to the outside peg or they can all use the same length of warp strands as the outside peg or weaving stick.

When you make smaller circles with thinner yarns on weaving sticks or thin pegs, the minimum working length for the warp strands at the center is 8" (20 cm). To make sure

you have enough length to tie the securing knot when the weaving is complete, don't cut the center lengths too short.

Weaving a Circle

1. Warp the loom according to the directions on page 8.

2. Next, set up the loom to weave circles. The radius of the circle is woven from the outside edge to the center, in rows that get shorter across the loom or weaving sticks. This shapes the weaving into a circle, and makes it look like it pivots from the right-hand side of the loom, because the rows at the right-hand side have the least amount of yarn on them. Place the center peg of the circle on the right side of the loom and the rest of the pegs to the left of it, ending with the peg that will be the outside edge of the circle at the left-hand side of the loom.

3. Weave the circle using the short row technique (see sidebar on page 36).

4. Continue, repeating the short row technique, advancing the weft on the left-hand side of the loom or weaving sticks until the outside circumference of the circle measures the desired length.

5. End the weaving by making a half hitch knot (see page 9) on the last peg. Snip the weft end.

When the pegs or weaving sticks are removed, the weaving will curve around.

Short Row Weaving

1. Beginning at the left side (the outside edge of the circle), leave a 2" (5 cm) tail of weft at the base of the first peg.

2. Make a half hitch loop (see page 9) with the tail end of the weft yarn and place it on the first peg. The yarn end will be woven in after the weaving is complete.

3. Weave 2 rows on all pegs.

4. Weave 2 rows on all pegs except the center peg (the right-hand edge peg).

5. Weave 2 rows skipping the 2 center pegs.

6. Continue to weave 2 row repeats that are each 1 peg shorter than the previous row by skipping 1 more peg at the right-hand side of the loom for each subsequent set of rows.

7. End by wrapping the left-hand edge peg once. This makes a wedge shape on the pegs, with only 2 rows of weaving at the center peg (right-hand side of the loom) and a number of rows that equals however many pegs you have chosen to be the radius of the circle. Advance the weft.

FINISHING

1. Ease the warp strands until the circle lies flat and the warp ends at the beginning of the weaving are about 4" (10 cm) to 6" (15 cm) long. The warp ends with the pegs still attached will be quite a bit longer.

2. Beginning at the center of the circle, tie knots in the warp ends to secure them.

3. Cut the warp yarns a couple inches from the knots and weave the warp ends into the channels.

4. Continue until all the warp ends are tied off and all the pegs are snipped from the weaving.

5. Weave in the weft ends at the beginning and end of the weaving.

Weaving a Circle with Two Pegs or Weaving Sticks

1. Warp 2 pegs or weaving sticks with 3 strands of #4 medium weight worsted yarn held together, for a working length of 12" (30 cm). The cut length is 24" (60 cm).

2. Place a half hitch knot (see page 9) on the left-hand peg or weaving stick.

3. Weave 1 row on 2 pegs.

4. Wrap the left-hand peg once.

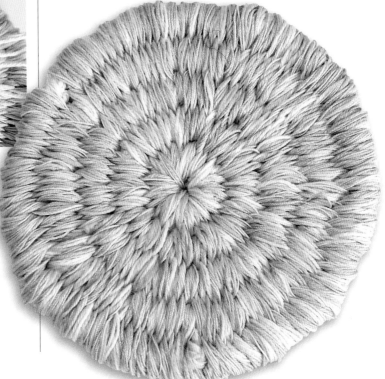

5. Repeat steps 3 and 4, weaving very densely and using a lot of weft.

6. For a 1" (2.5 cm)-diameter circle, weave until you have 3" (7.5 cm) of very densely woven fabric on the left-hand peg or weaving stick. For a 2" (5 cm)-diameter circle, weave until there is 6" (15 cm) of very densely woven fabric on the left-hand peg or weaving stick. Snip the weft end from the ball of yarn.

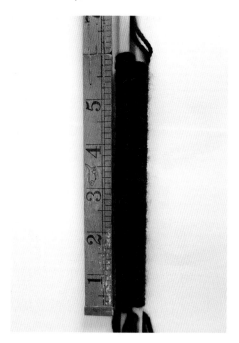

7. Ease the weaving down the weaving sticks.

8. Pull up the warp strands on the right-hand (center of the circle) weaving stick or peg very firmly to close the center of the circle, and then tie a knot. Snip the weaving sticks from the warp strands. The circle will be ruffled and distorted at this point.

9. Weave the ends into the center channel and trim.

10. Ease the circle flat while pulling up on the outside warp ends. Then take half the warp ends over and under the ones from the other end of the channel to make a partial knot.

11. Thread the warp strands from one end of the channel into a craft needle that has a very large eye or a latch hook. Thread the warp strands into the outside channel. Each set of warp ends will go in the opposite direction from the other, away from the partial knot. It's easiest to thread the ends into the channel in stages, a few ends at a time.

12. If the partial knot needs to be concealed, then stitch over it with some of the weft ends before weaving them in.

How to Weave a Pinwheel Circle

Pinwheel circles are woven with two or more colors of weft yarn. The pinwheel circle begins at the right-hand side of the loom or weaving sticks, which is the center of the circle, because the color changes are made at the center of the circle. When color changes are made at the edge of the right-hand weaving stick or peg, there are no long floats along the outside edge. If the color changes are done at the left-hand or outside edge of the circle, there will be long floats of the color(s) that is not being woven. Traveling passes are made to keep the color changes at the right-hand side and move the weft across so the center shaping can begin.

WEAVING

Note: You can make the pinwheel circle with as many colors of weft as you want. If you decide to use more than two colors in the pinwheel circle, add them at the center and weave in the same manner as weaving with just two colors.

1. Warp the loom according to the directions on page 8.

2. Beginning at the right-hand side (the center of the circle), tie 2 colors of yarn together, leaving a 2" (5 cm) tail of weft at the base of the first peg. The yarn ends will be woven in after the weaving is complete.

3. With color 1: Make a *traveling pass*. This means that you weave from the right-hand side to the left-hand edge of the loom or weaving sticks. The rows will now end at the left-hand side of the loom.

Weave 2 rows on all pegs. (Notice that I've pushed the warp strands out of the way for the purposes of clarity in the photos.)

Weave 2 rows on all pegs except the center peg (the right-hand edge peg).

Weave 2 rows, skipping the 2 center pegs.

Continue to weave 2-row repeats that are each 1 peg shorter than the previous row by skipping 1 more peg at the middle for each subsequent set of rows.

End by wrapping the left-hand edge peg once. You will now have a wedge shape on the pegs, with only 2 rows of weaving at the center peg and a number of rows that equals however many pegs you have chosen to be the radius of the circle. (Notice that the rows of weft are spread apart in the photo to show the weaving sequence more clearly.)

4. Advance the warp.

Make a second traveling pass to take the weft back to the center of the circle, which is the right-hand peg, for the color change. Weave across all the pegs or weaving sticks from the left to the right-hand side.

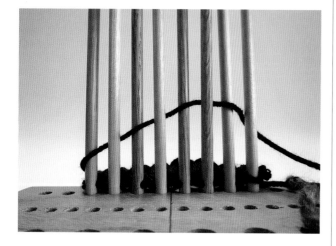

Color change: Drop color 1 and bring color 2 under it.

5. Repeat steps 2–4 until the circle is complete.

Tip Always take the previous color under the working color to lock the center and remember to advance the warp between color changes so each wedge begins with the long rows flat across the lower edge of the loom.

FINISHING

1. Ease the warp strands until the circle lies flat and the warp ends at the starting edge are about 3" (7.5 cm) long.

2. Beginning at the center, tie knots in the warp ends to secure them.

3. Cut the warp yarns a few inches from the knots.

4. Weave the warp ends into the channels.

5. Weave in the weft ends at the beginning and end of the weaving.

Pillbox Hat

The Pillbox Hat shown here with the Mobius Cowl.

A pillbox hat is a quick and easy project, woven in only two pieces. The crown of the hat is a circle, and the sides are a long strip that is joined at the center back and then stitched to the crown. Weaving the hat with self-striping or patterned yarn adds extra pizzazz. An alternate version can be woven with two colors of yarn. If you need to make a smaller version, make the top with fewer pegs to make it smaller and weave the side panel shorter. If you want a larger hat, add more pegs to make a larger circle and weave a longer panel for the sides of the hat.

Equipment

- Dewberry Ridge 6" (15 cm)-wide peg loom or a loom of your choice
- 12 pegs, ¼" (6 mm) in diameter
- tape measure
- scissors
- warp threader
- blunt tapestry needle
- latch hook

Yarn

- Warp: #4 medium weight acrylic yarn, 2 balls, 1.7 oz./50 g each
- Weft: Unique by Lion Brand (100% acrylic; 3.5 oz./100 g, 109 yd./100 m), #210 Circus, 1 ball

Specs

- WPI: 9 wraps per 1" (2.5 cm)
- Finished Measurements: Approximately 7½" (18.75 cm) in diameter by about 3" (7.5 cm) high

Notes

The Pillbox Hat is woven with 1 strand of yarn for the weft. The warp is 2 strands of yarn held together.

Crown

SETUP

The circle for the crown of the Pillbox Hat is woven on 8 pegs. To set up the warp strands:

- The working length of the warp strands is 36" (90 cm), so the cut length of the warp strands before threading them into the pegs is 72" (180 cm) for the pegs at the outside of the circle (the left-hand side of the circle).
- The warp strands at the center of the circle (the right-hand side of the loom) can be as short as 8" (20 cm) working length, but no shorter, and they can be longer if you prefer. The remaining 7 pegs between the right-hand edge and left-hand edge can have the warp strands gradually getting longer until they reach 36" (90 cm) working length.

WEAVING

Weave the circle. See How to Weave a Circle on page 35.

FINISHING

Tie square knots all the way across: left over right and under, right over left and under, pull up. Weave in the ends.

Sides

SETUP

1. The side panel of the Pillbox Hat is woven on 6 pegs.

2. Set up the warp: The working length of the warp strands is 36" (90 cm), so the cut length of the warp strands before threading into the pegs is 72" (180 cm).

WEAVING

1. Thread the warp strands into the pegs and weave 24" (60 cm). The side section should be very firm, so weave in a lot of weft and pack it densely.

2. Distribute the weft evenly along the warp strands, making sure you have 6" (15 cm) of warp for finishing at both ends of the weaving.

3. Bring the ends of the weaving together. Carefully line up the channels so they match.

4. Tie square knots all the way across: left over right and under, right over left and under, pull up.

FINISHING

1. On the side panel, weave half the strands into the channels to one side of the knots and the other half into the channels on the other side of the knots.

2. Pin the crown in place and then stitch the sides to the crown.

Two-Color Pillbox Hat

The Two-Color Pillbox Hat uses the same materials and is woven in the same way as the Pillbox Hat, but uses two colors of yarn. Weave with two strands of the same color yarn held together.

Yarn

- Warp: #4 medium weight acrylic yarn, 2 balls, 1.7 oz./50 g each
- Weft: Kitchen Cotton by Lion Brand (100% cotton; 2 oz./57 g, 99 yd./90 m), #147 Grape and #114 Cayenne, 1 ball each

WEAVING

1. Weave the top of the Two-Color Pillbox Hat by following the instructions for a pinwheel circle on page 39.

2. Weave the side panel in geometric patterns following the instructions on page 136, using 7 pegs instead of 6 pegs, as the diamond pattern requires an odd number of pegs.

FINISHING

Finish the Two-Color Pillbox Hat in the same way as the Pillbox Hat.

Blessing Basket

ometimes life gives you a little gift that feels like a blessing, a treasure. It's lovely to have a special little nest to place that blessing in—a Blessing Basket. You can hold it in your hand or place it on a windowsill.

The Blessing Basket is very easy to weave. It begins as a circle woven with one, two, or three colors.

To form the base of the Blessing Basket, the inner half of the circle is finished so it lies flat. Then, the basket is formed by pulling up on the warp strands on the two outside weaving sticks. This motion compresses the channels of weaving and forces the sides of the basket to lift out of the circle, rather like the way that your heart does when a sudden blessing arrives in your life.

Embellishing the Blessing Basket is the time to let your creativity shine. Consider adding yarn babies or woven buttons, hearts, circles, or squares. Or you can add found objects from nature or buttons, beads, charms, and other ephemera you find at a thrift shop or yard sale. Experiment, and perhaps add a handle.

Any yarn and even non-yarns will work well for this project. Use hand-spun, art yarn, T-shirt yarn, or fabric strips. Non-fiber choices might include plastic cord, tape, or paper torn into strips. The sky is the limit when it comes to materials.

One of the best tips I can give you is to look for color inspiration in unusual places. As I was writing the instructions for the Blessing Basket, a dear friend sent me a photo of a California red-sided garter snake. She thought that the colors and textures would be fabulous in one of my knitted designs. I agreed but found it far more inspiring to weave a Blessing Basket using the vibrant hues of this gentle and gloriously beautiful creature. The finished basket celebrates a friendship that has endured for decades.

The finished size of your Blessing Basket is determined by the size of the weaving sticks, the thickness of the weft, and the number and thickness of the warp strands you use. The Blessing Baskets I've designed are not meant to be huge; rather, they are meant to weave the feelings of gratitude and love into a small, tender, and heartfelt celebration of life and all its wonders. If you want a tinier than usual basket, choose thin yarns and fine weaving sticks.

Equipment

- Dewberry Ridge 10" (25 cm) weaving sticks
  - For thick to bulky weight yarns: ½" (1.3 cm)-diameter
  - For medium to bulky weight yarns: ⅜" (9 mm)-diameter
  - For medium weight yarns: ¼" (6 mm)-diameter
- steel weaving sticks from Daegrad Tools (2 sets of 4 sticks), ⅛" (3 mm) in diameter, or any size you prefer
- tape measure
- scissors
- warp threader
- blunt tapestry needle
- latch hook

Yarn

- Warp: #4 medium weight acrylic yarn, 3 balls, 1.7 oz./50 g each
- Weft:
  - For weaving sticks ½" (1.3 cm) in diameter: bulky weight yarn, Super by Briggs & Little (100% pure wool; 4 oz./113 g, 85 yd./77 m), #73 Red, #41 Navy Blue, and #45 Peacock, 1 ball each
  - For weaving sticks ⅜" (9 mm) in diameter: T-shirt yarn with a strand of multicolor thread held together
  - For weaving sticks ¼" (6 mm) in diameter: medium weight yarn, Atlantic by Briggs & Little (100% pure wool; 4 oz./113 g, 135 yd./128 m), #30 Fern and #44 Teal, 1 ball each
  - For weaving sticks ⅛" (3 mm) in diameter: lace weight yarn hand spun from Nomad Fibreworks or any T-shirt yarn, cord, string, yarns, and threads that you prefer
  - For the Upcycled Blessing Basket (⅜" [9 mm]-diameter weaving sticks): stretch wrap packing tape (nonadhesive)

Left to right: The circles for the bottoms of the baskets woven on ½" (1.25 cm), ⅜" (9 mm), ¼" (6 mm), and ⅛" (3 mm) weaving sticks.

Specs

- WPI: Varies
- Finished Measurements:
  - The Blessing Basket woven on ½" (1.25 cm)-diameter weaving sticks is approximately 6" (15 cm) in diameter and 3" (7.5 cm) tall. The woven circle is 9" (22.5 cm) in diameter when lying flat.
  - The Blessing Basket woven on the ⅜" (9 mm)-diameter weaving sticks is approximately 1½" (3.75 cm) tall and 5" (12.5 cm) in diameter. The woven circle is 5½" (13.75 cm) in diameter when lying flat.
  - The Blessing Basket woven on ¼" (6 mm)-diameter weaving sticks is approximately 3½" (8.75 cm) in diameter and 1½" (3.75 cm) tall. The woven circle is 5¼" (13.5 cm) in diameter when lying flat.
  - The Blessing Basket woven on ⅛" (3 mm)-diameter weaving sticks is approximately 1¾" (4.5 cm) in diameter and 1" (2.5 cm) tall. The woven circle is 3" (7.5 cm) in diameter when lying flat.
  - The Upcycled Blessing Basket, which was woven on ⅜" (9 mm)-diameter weaving sticks, is approximately 5" (12.5 cm) in diameter and 1½" (3.75 cm) tall. The woven circle is 7½" (18.75 cm) in diameter when lying flat.

Notes

The Upcycled Blessing Basket was made from nonadhesive stretch wrap tape we bought when we were moving. Once it has been used, then rolled into a ball, the tape wants to act like twine or yarn and squishes into a strand that is bulky weight. I used one layer of the tape as yarn when weaving the Upcycled Blessing Basket. We saved all of the tape for upcycling projects. It's supposed to be 100 percent biodegradable, so the basket woven with it may have a short lifespan. We shall see . . .

Above: This basket was woven with T-shirt yarn held together with a multicolor thread on ⅜" (9 mm)-diameter weaving sticks.

Above: This basket was woven with bulky weight yarn on ½" (1.25 cm)-diameter weaving sticks.

Right: The Upcycled Blessing Basket was woven with nonadhesive packing tape on ⅜" (9 mm)-diameter weaving sticks.

Above: You can weave with some unconventional materials—even nonadhesive wrap tape, as in the Upcycled Blessing Basket. Don't be afraid to give something unusual a try!

Above: This basket was woven with medium weight yarn on ¼" (6 mm)-diameter weaving sticks.

Left: This basket was woven with hand-spun yarn on ⅛" (3 mm)-diameter weaving sticks.

SETUP

For the ¼" (6 mm)-diameter weaving sticks, warp 6 sticks with 2 strands of yarn. The working length of the left-hand outside edge weaving stick warp strands is 27"/67.5 cm long (cut length 54"/135 cm).

For the ½" (1.25 cm)-diameter weaving sticks, warp 6 weaving sticks with 3 strands of yarn held together. The working length of the left-hand outside edge weaving stick warp strands is 40" (100 cm) long. The cut length is 80" (200 cm).

For the ⅜" (9 mm)- and ¼" (6 mm)-diameter weaving sticks, warp 6 weaving sticks with 2 strands of yarn held together. The working length of the left-hand outside edge weaving stick warp strands is 40" (100 cm) long. The cut length is 80" (200 cm).

For the ⅛" (3 mm) weaving sticks, warp 6 weaving sticks with 1 strand of yarn. The working length of the left-hand outside edge weaving stick is 18" (45 cm). The cut length is 24" (60 cm).

WEAVING

Following the instructions on page 38, weave a circle with 6 weaving sticks.

FINISHING

1. Untie the knot in the weft strands at the beginning of the weaving.

2. Ease the warp strands until the center 4 channels of the circle lie flat and the warp ends at the beginning of the weaving are about 4" (10 cm) to 6" (15 cm) long.

3. Beginning at the center of the circle, form the base.
Tie knots in the warp ends to secure them.
Cut the warp yarns a couple of inches from the knot.
Weave the warp ends into the channels and trim the ends.
Repeat these steps on the next 3 center weaving sticks so the warp ends on the center 4 weaving sticks are tied

off and the 4 center weaving sticks are snipped from the weaving.

4. Form the sides. Pull up the warp strands on the outside 2 weaving sticks to lift the sides up from the base of the basket.

5. Experiment with the shaping of the basket. When you are pleased with it, tie off the warp strands, cut the warp strands from the weaving sticks, and weave in the ends. Weave in the weft ends at the beginning and end of the weaving. Embellish the Blessing Basket in any way that feels right to you.

Three-Color Blessing Basket

To weave a Three-Color Blessing Basket, follow the instructions for weaving a pinwheel circle on page 39, using 3 colors of weft instead of 2. The weaving stick at the right-hand edge (the center of the basket) can have shorter warp strands, but don't go any shorter than 10" (25 cm). The weaving sticks between the two edges can all be the same length as the left-hand weaving stick or, if you prefer, you can stagger their lengths, making each one a few inches shorter. Following the instructions on page 39, tie the ends of the weft strands together and place them at the right-hand side of the weaving sticks. Alternating the colors, weave a pinwheel circle.

Shape and finish the basket as instructed for the Blessing Basket on page 48.

Brooches

Brooches are so much fun to make—and are quite useful, too. They are handy for holding vests and shawls closed and scarves in place. They are great for pure and simple embellishment—on a basket, a hat, a bag, a cowl, or a lapel. Brooches can be woven with any kind of yarn, whether it's hand-spun or art yarn, string, cord, paper strips, fabric strips, or random balls of crochet cotton rescued from thrift shops.

The finished size of the brooch is determined by the size of weaving sticks and thickness of weft that you use. Weaving a small circle is an excellent way to swatch a larger project, as it gives a good indication of how the yarn will interact with the pegs or weaving sticks. But the swatch can be more than a swatch—it can continue its life as a pretty little pin.

WEAVING

With your choice of yarn and weaving sticks, weave a small circle as instructed on page 35.

FINISHING

Back the brooch with a pin back or stitch on a safety pin for closure. Safety pins are especially good for larger pins that are going to be used to hold heavier shawls and scarves in place.

Painted Circles

I have a secret addiction: I can't resist "rescuing" balls of unloved crochet cotton in thrift shops. They have a habit of mounting up, which can be a space-gobbling problem. My favorite way of dealing with this built-up stash is to hold lots of strands of old crochet cotton together as if they were one strand and then weave circles with it to create "blank canvases" I can paint on to use as buttons, brooches, and masks or faces.

Yes, you can paint on your weaving if you use the right materials! Weave small circles (see page 35 for directions) using six or seven strands of white or cream-colored crochet cotton held together, and then paint them with acrylic paint. The paints in the photos are by Jacquard, but other brands will work as well.

Buttons

Buttons are a treat to weave. They are quick and easy, and they solve the dilemma of how to find the perfect button to match your project. They are also a wonderful way to showcase art yarns and hand-spun treasures. The finished size of the button will be determined by the diameter of the weaving sticks, the thickness of the weft yarn, and the number and thickness of the warp strands.

SETUP

1. Warp 2 pegs with 3 strands of #4 medium weight worsted yarn held together, for a working (folded) length of 12" (30 cm); unfolded length is 24" (60 cm).

2. Place a half hitch knot on the left-hand peg or weaving stick.

WEAVING

1. Weave 1 row on 2 pegs (like a figure 8). Wrap the left-hand peg once.

2. Repeat step 1, weaving very densely and using a lot of weft, until your button reaches the desired diameter. (The circumference of the circle is three times the diameter, so just weave three times as long as what you want the button to measure across.)

For a 2" (5 cm)-diameter button, weave until you have 6" (15 cm) of densely woven material on the left-hand peg or weaving stick.

3. Ease the weaving down the weaving sticks until there is an equal amount of warp on each end of the weaving. Snip the center peg from the warp strands.

FINISHING

1. Pull up the warp strands on the right-hand side (center of the circle) very firmly to close the center of the circle, and then tie a knot. The circle will be ruffled and distorted at this point.

2. Do not trim the warp ends yet. Leave at least 5" (12.5 cm) warp ends hanging from the center knot so you can sew the button to another object. (See page 33 for instructions on how to stitch a woven button to a project.)

3. Weave one set of warp ends into the center channel and bring them out halfway around the circle, staying in the inside channel.

4. Ease the circle flat while pulling up on the outside warp ends. Then take half the warp ends over and under the ones from the other end of the outside channel to make a partial knot.

5. Snip the warp ends a few inches from the partial knot.

6. Thread the warp strands from one end of the channel into a craft needle that has a very large eye and then into the outside channel. Each set of warp ends will go in the opposite direction away from the partial knot.

> *Tip* If the ends are challenging to thread into the channel, thread them in stages, a few ends at a time. If the partial knot needs to be concealed, stitch over it with some of the weft ends before taking them into the channel.

Masks

The circle is a very good place to begin to create a mask. Start by drawing circles and doodling all kinds of shapes in them. Think of new ways to suggest eyes, nose, mouth, and ears. Google or check out Pinterest to find vintage or historical masks. Fascinating!

Here are some things to think about as you get started:

- What shapes can you use to creatively represent the human face?
- What colors will suggest different emotions?
- How have other cultures made masks?

Tip For an in-depth look at woven masks, check out the work of master weaver Susan Barrett Merrill of weavingalife.com/. Her masks are sublime and awe inspiring. Her masks can be admired at susanbarrettmerrill.com/.

A woven circle is the foundation for a mask, but the sky is the limit on embellishments.

Preliminary doodles for mask ideas.

The face on this mask was burned onto driftwood, and the circle was embellished with driftwood, sea glass, and beads.

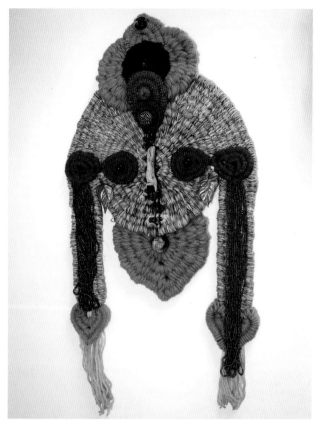

This circle is embellished with half hitch cords and beads.

Combine circles, petal shapes (see page 78), hearts (see page 86), and a narrow band for this mask. It was woven with many different yarns and embellished with beads, buttons, and found objects.

WEAVING

Refer to the instructions on how to weave circles on page 35.

FINISHING

Finish the circle as instructed on page 35, and embellish as you choose.

Circular Vest

The Circular Vest is woven in three pieces: two narrow curved side panels and one rectangular center back panel. The side panels are woven with a short row technique, which forms semicircles that radiate out from the armhole edge. The template will ensure that the shape is just right. The side sections are stitched to the back panel. The sides fold over at the neck and throat to create a flattering shawl collar. The vest is flattering to all body shapes.

Equipment

- 12" (30 cm)-wide peg loom or a loom of your choice
- 24 medium-size pegs, ¼" (6 mm) in diameter
- tape measure
- scissors
- warp threader
- blunt tapestry needle
- long glass top pins or T-pins
- large sewing needle and heavy-duty thread
- ruler
- pencil or pen
- heavy brown paper
- latch hook
- steam iron and cushion or ironing board

Yarn

- Warp: #4 medium weight acrylic yarn, 2 balls, 1.7 oz./50 g each
- Weft:
  - Hand-painted Softspun by Briggs & Little (100% pure wool; 4 oz./113 g, 240 yd./219 m), #28 Black Magic, 2 balls for accent color
  - Atlantic by Briggs & Little (100% pure wool; 4 oz./113 g, 135 yd./123 m), #16 Black, 1 ball for background color for the center back panel; #19 Seafoam, 2 balls for background color for the side panels

Specs

- WPI: Softspun, 9 wraps per 1" (2.5 cm); Atlantic, 8 wraps per 1" (2.5 cm)
- Finished Measurements: This vest is sized for medium (approximately 12–14). When laid flat and opened out, the center back is approximately 27" (67.5 cm) long and the measurement from the center of the front lapel curved edge to the other lapel edge is 40" (100 cm). The vest folds to have a collar and lapels, so the size is quite flexible and fits a broad range of body types, but for more voluptuous figures it will be necessary to increase the measurements of the vest.
- The best way to work out the correct size for you is to enlarge the template on page 59 and then cut out a sample vest in muslin or waste fabric.
  - To make the vest smaller, weave with 14–16 pegs for the side panels and 18–20 pegs for the center back panel.
  - To make it larger, weave with 28–36 pegs (depending on how much larger you would prefer vest to be) for the side panels and 28–36 pegs for the center panel.
  - If you are tall, weave the center back panel longer.

Notes

Remember that 1 pass (weaving from one side of the loom to the other) is half of a row. To weave a full row, you must weave from one side to the other and back to the beginning point. The vertical stripes pattern in the back section is formed by weaving 1 pass of background color and 1 pass of accent color for each full row.

SETUP

Make the template by scaling up the pattern (see page 59) on heavy paper.

WEAVING THE CENTER BACK PANEL (MAKE 1)

1. Warp 24 medium ¼" (6 mm) pegs with warp strands with a working length of 36" (90 cm) long.

2. Weave 4 rows with background color for the border.

3. Create the vertical stripes pattern: Make 1 pass with background color and then 1 pass with accent color to complete 1 row. See page 132, How to Weave Vertical Stripes, for more instruction.

4. Continue creating vertical stripes for 23½" (58.75 cm), then weave 4 rows of background color.

5. Advance the warp until you have 6" (15 cm) warp strands at both ends of the weaving. Snip the pegs from the warp strands and work a double Damascus edge (see page 17) at both ends of the center back panel. Weave the warp ends into the weaving.

Circular Vest Template

Neck Edge

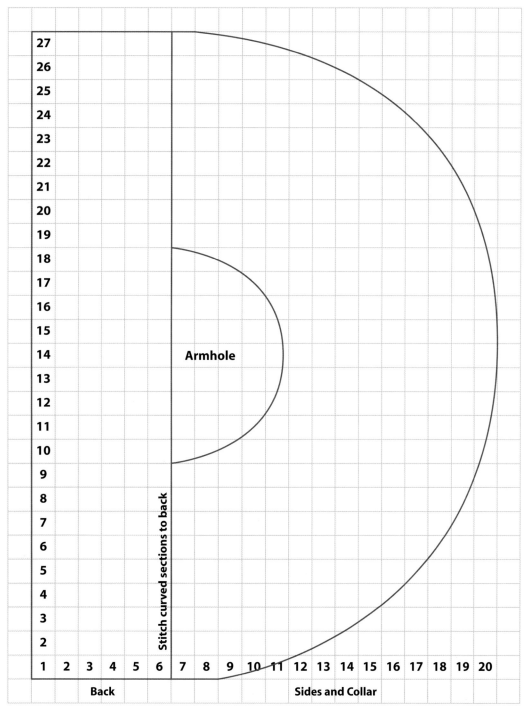

Center Back Fold

27
26
25
24
23
22
21
20
19
18
17
16
15
14   Armhole
13
12
11
10
9
8
7   Stitch curved sections to back
6
5
4
3
2
1   2   3   4   5   6   7   8   9   10 11 12 13 14 15 16 17 18 19 20

Front Edge

Back   **Sides and Collar**

Lower Edge

WEAVING THE SIDE PANELS (MAKE 2)

These steps will create a vertical stripe pattern on the left-hand side of the weaving and a background color strip that has only half as much weft in it, creating the curve.

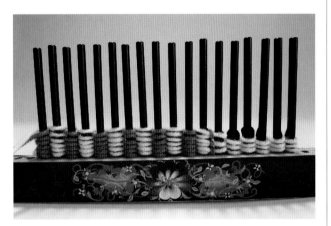

1. Warp 18 medium ¼" (6 mm) pegs with warp strands with a working length of 54" (135 cm) long.

2. Tie the background color and accent color together. Begin on the left-hand side of the loom by holding the knot against the left-hand edge peg. (*Note:* In the photos, the accent color is the pink yarn and the background color is white. Normally, the warp yarns would extend out behind the loom, but for clarity, they have been pushed to the side.)

3. Take the accent color to the front of the left-hand edge peg and weave to the right over 12 pegs. Stop 6 pegs from the right-hand side.

4. Bring the yarn to the front of the loom, leaving 6 pegs at the right-hand side of the loom empty.

5. Take the background color behind the first peg on the left-hand side. Weave all the way across from left to right and then weave back from right to left over 5 pegs. Bring the yarn to the front of the loom 1 peg over from where the accent color is parked.

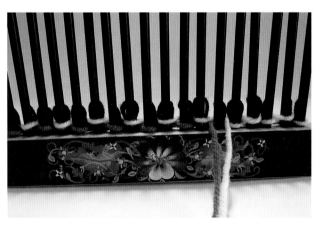

6. Change yarns. Take the accent color over the background color and to the back of the loom. Leave the strand of background color parked in front of the loom. It gets pulled up by the accent color and now covers the front of the sixth peg. *Note:* Taking the accent color over the background color is essential to keeping the continuity. It will create a little vertical line of accent color.

7. Weave the accent color back to the left-hand side of the loom, following the same path as on the first pass. Drop the accent color. This step will form the vertical line of accent color.

8. Pick up the background color and weave to the left-hand side of the loom, being sure to weave it in the same path it traveled previously to maintain the vertical stripes.

9. Repeat steps 3–8 for 42" (105 cm), measured on the left-hand side (the outside edge of the panel; the solid color edge at the right-hand side is the armhole edge).

Tip When beginning the pattern repeat, the accent color yarn must go under the background color at the left-hand side to lock it in place at the edge.

FINISHING

1. When the weaving is complete, lift it off the loom and lay it on the template. Advance the warp strands, moving the weaving into place on the template. Work a double Damascus edge (see page 17) along the ends of the weaving. Weave the ends in.

2. Steam the 3 pieces of the vest and ease them out to the full measurements of the template. Block them by pinning them to a cushion or ironing board until they are completely dry.

3. Place the vest pieces on the template. Line up the side panels and stitch them to the center back panel.

Collar Statement Necklace

The woven Collar Statement Necklace can be worn on its own or embellished with woven brooches (see page 50). Wear it with the fastening at the back or the front. For added pizzazz, try embellishing the Collar Statement Necklace with charms, beads, buttons, or found objects. The finished size of the necklace is determined by the size of the weaving sticks and thickness of the yarn or threads, roving, ribbon, cord, T-shirt yarn, or whatever you decide to use for weft. Adding or subtracting weaving sticks or pegs will also change the finished size of the necklace.

My suggestion is to weave the necklace in black (or your choice of color) and an accent color. The short row technique creates a curved striped pattern on the left-hand side of the weaving and a black stripe that has only half as much weft in it at the neck edge, creating the curve.

Equipment

- weaving sticks or a peg loom of your choice (I used 2 looms: a 3" [7.5 cm]-wide peg loom with white pegs—Daisy Hill Handiworks model PL 133 with ¼" [6 mm] pegs set at ½" [1.3 cm] on center; and a 4" [10 cm]-wide peg loom with black pegs—Daisy Hill Handiworks model PL 127 with ⅜" [9 mm] pegs set at 1" [2.5 cm] on center.)
- tape measure
- scissors
- warp threader
- blunt tapestry needle
- needle and thread
- closure or fastener
- steam iron and cushion or ironing board
- compass, pencils, and paper to make template

Yarn

- Warp: #4 medium weight acrylic yarn, 2 balls, 1.7 oz./50 g each
- Weft:
  - Unique by Lion Brand, #5 bulky weight (100% acrylic; 3.5 oz./100 g, 109 yd./100 m), #201 Garden, 1 ball for accent color
  - Vanna's Choice by Lion Brand, #4 medium weight (100% acrylic; 3.5 oz./100 g, 170 yd./156 m), Black, 1 ball
  - Handspun: 4 oz./113 g Turquoise Medley, for accent color
  - Handspun: 4 oz./113 g Black/Firestar Medley, for accent color

Specs

- WPI: 9 wraps per 1" (2.5 cm)
- Finished Measurements:
  - Medium: Approximately 30" (75 cm) in circumference at the outside edge
  - Large: Approximately 36" (90 cm) in circumference at the outside edge
  - Medium: 9" (22.5 cm) in diameter
  - Large: 11" (27.5 cm) in diameter

Notes

Draw a circle that is 4" (10 cm) in diameter for a medium-size neck opening. The necklaces in the photos are sized for a medium-size neck, so if you want the Collar Statement Necklace to be larger, draw a circle that is 5" (12.5 cm) in diameter.

SETUP

Warp 6 pegs or weaving sticks with warp strands with a working length of 45" (112.5 cm) long. The cut length is 90" (225 cm).

WEAVING

1. Use 1 strand of weft when working with ¼" (6 mm) pegs. Use 2 strands of weft held together when working with ⅜" (9 mm) pegs.

2. Tie the black and accent color weft yarns together. Begin on the left-hand side of the loom by holding the knot at the left-hand edge peg.

3. Take the accent color to the front of the left-hand edge peg and weave to the right over 4 pegs. Stop 2 pegs from the right-hand side.

4. Bring the yarn to the front of the loom, leaving 2 pegs at the right-hand side of the loom empty.

5. Take the black yarn behind the first peg on the left-hand side. Gently tug it to move the knot to the back of the loom so it sits between the first and second pegs from the left-hand side. This step will create a clean finish on the hem of the Collar Statement Necklace.

6. Weave across all 6 pegs or weaving sticks from left to right, then bring the black yarn around the right-hand peg to the front of the loom.

7. Take the black yarn *over* the accent color.

8. Change yarns: Lift the accent color up, catching the black yarn. The black yarn is now pulled in front of the peg that is second from the right-hand edge of the loom. This step makes a little vertical stitch of accent color.

9. Take the accent color back through the space between the fourth and fifth pegs and weave back to the left-hand side of the loom, following the same path as the first pass. Drop the accent color.

10. Pick up the black yarn and take it over the accent color.

11. Tug it gently to move the loop of accent color yarn to the space between the first and second pegs at the back of the loom. This step wraps the left-hand peg completely in the accent color.

12. Here's how the back looks: The loom is flipped upside down in this photo to show how the first peg is covered by a loop of the accent color because of the tugging of the black. The result is 2 channels of accent color on the back. The front still has the alternating black and accent stripes.

13. Bring the black yarn to the front and weave to the left-hand side of the loom, being sure to weave it in the same path it traveled previously to maintain the color stripes.

14. Repeat steps 3–13 for 40" (100 cm), measured on the left-hand side. (*Note:* The solid color edge at the right-hand side is the neck edge.)

Tip By pulling on the black yarn to move the accent color around and to the back of the left-hand peg, the hem of the Collar Statement Necklace will have a clean finish at the edge. Note that when beginning the pattern repeat, the accent color yarn must go under the background color at the left-hand side to make a loop for the black yarn to pull the colored loop back and lock it in place at the back of the left-hand peg.

FINISHING

1. When the weaving is complete, lift it off the loom and lay it around the circle template. Advance the warp strands, moving the weaving into place so the edges of the Collar Statement Necklace come together and the opening fits the circle template.

2. Work a double Damascus edge (see page 17) along both ends of the weaving. Weave the ends in.

3. Stitch a closure onto the necklace.

CHAPTER 5

Squares and Other Shapes

Squares are the building blocks for many unique projects. Weaving a square on a peg loom or weaving sticks can be challenging, but I've worked out some techniques that will have you making squares in no time. Work your way through the technique section, then move on to baskets, brooches, hearts, and some decorative weaving art projects.

How to Weave a Square

I was convinced that it had to be possible to weave peg loom squares that have finished edges with no warp strands at the edge. After a lot of trial and error, I developed a solid method, and I was ecstatic when I had finally figured it out. My method makes it possible to weave nifty different size squares using an odd number of weaving sticks or pegs on a peg loom, which means the design potential is unlimited.

The finished size of the squares depends on the size of your peg loom or weaving sticks, the thickness of yarn or other fibers, and the number of pegs or weaving sticks that you use for the square. Peg looms with more pegs will allow you to weave larger squares, but even small peg looms will yield several different sizes of squares.

The squares work great as hot pads, place mats, or seat cushions and can be stitched together to make baskets, bags, shawls, blankets, rugs, and throws. They are a universally useful shape!

The Basics

Squares are woven using a short row technique (see page 36) to form four triangles. The top point of each triangle meets in the center of the square when the warp strands are pulled up at the end of the weaving.

The spacing of pegs varies among loom builders and even in different models of looms from the same builder. This difference will affect the final size of the woven piece, so you may need to experiment to find the perfect number of pegs or weaving sticks and the right thickness of weft to weave the size of square you wish to make.

The squares in the photos were woven with seven weaving sticks.

Determining the Working Length of the Warp Strands

1. Figure out the length of each side of the square. Measure the distance from the left-hand peg to the right-hand peg on the loom (or the width of the 7 weaving sticks held slightly apart from each other) and multiple it by 2.

2. Multiply the length of the side of your square by 4 and add 12" (30 cm). This will be the working length of the warp strands for the left-hand side of the peg loom or weaving sticks (the outside edge of the square).

3. To find the working length of the remaining warp strands for the inner rounds and the center of the square, reduce the length of warp on the remaining pegs or weaving sticks in steps to about 12" (30 cm).

Tip If you are planning to make several squares and don't want to worry about doing the math or figuring out the various working warp strand lengths, here's a quick trick. Simply cut all of your warp strands for all the weaving sticks or pegs to the same length as the longest, outside edge peg or weaving stick.

WEAVING

Before you begin, be sure you understand the orientation of the triangle shapes on the peg loom or weaving sticks. The center of the square (the top of the triangle) is on the right-hand side of the peg loom or weaving sticks, and the long outside edge is at the left-hand side of the peg loom or weaving sticks. The following directions apply to peg looms or weaving sticks.

1. Start the weaving at the left-hand side of the peg loom. Leave a 6" (15 cm) tail of weft at the base of the first peg on the left-hand edge.

2. Make 4 half hitch knots (see page 9) on the first peg on the left-hand side of the peg loom.

3. Weave 4 rows on the first 2 pegs on the left-hand side of the peg loom.

4. Weave a set of 4 rows at a time from the left-hand peg working toward the right-hand side, weaving with 1 more peg each set until you have woven to the center of the peg loom.

5. Center row: Weave 2 rows on all pegs.

6. Shape the second half of the triangle wedge: Weave the remaining second half of the triangular wedge by weaving 4 rows at a time, working with one less peg on the right-hand side every time you complete 4 rows. Continue up to the last peg on the left-hand side of the peg loom. Work 4 half hitches on the last peg on the left-hand side.

7. Advance the weft when needed, as determined by the height of your pegs and when you have worked from steps 3–6, which completes 1 triangular wedge shape.

8. Repeat steps 3–7 three more times, completing 4 triangle wedges in total.

9. Snip the weft end, leaving a tail of 6" (15 cm).

FINISHING

1. Ease the warp strands all the way through the weaving so you have warp strands at the beginning and end of the weaving.

2. Beginning at the center of the square, pull up on the warp ends and tie square knots (see page 10) with the warp ends to secure them. Match the warp ends carefully to make sure you are tying the knot in the same channel and not to the neighboring warp strands. As you tie the knots, push on the weft strands with your fingers to move them into a square shape of the desired size.

3. Weave half the warp ends into the channels on one side of the knots; then, weave the remaining half of the warp strands into the channels on the other side of the knots. At the center, you will probably have to take the ends through the weaving several times to secure.

How to Weave a Small Square on Three Weaving Sticks or Pegs

1. Place a half hitch on the first peg on the left-hand side. Wrap the left-hand peg three times.

2. Weave 4 rows on 2 pegs.

3. Weave 3 rows on 3 pegs.

4. Weave 4 rows on 2 pegs.

5. Wrap the left-hand peg three times.

6. Repeat steps 2–5 three more times.

FINISHING

Finish the small square in the same way as the larger square.

Small woven squares work beautifully as brooches. The size of your weaving sticks or pegs and the thickness of your yarn will determine the size of the finished brooch. The small brooch was woven on ⅛" (3 mm)-diameter weaving sticks from Daegrad Tools. The large brooch was woven on ¼" (6 mm)-diameter weaving sticks from Daisy Hill Handiworks.

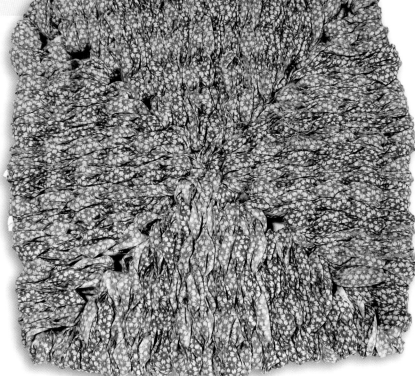

A square woven from fabric strips makes a comfy chair pad.

Circles and Squares Rug

People often have the mistaken idea that you need to have a large loom to be able to weave rugs. *Wrong.* Wonderful rugs can be created with the smallest of peg looms or with weaving sticks. Who says that a rug has to be solid weaving? Why not make a whimsical rug that is a fun combination of shapes that are stitched together? In this rug, I've stitched together circles and squares in a celebration of geometry.

The secret to putting it all together? Cut out a piece of heavy-duty paper as a template and pin the shapes to it so you can be sure that you are happy with the placement of the elements.

Remember that the edges of the rug do not have to be exactly straight and the shapes can be placed past the side edges of the template, if you wish.

Also remember that your rug does *not* have to be a rectangle. Make it any shape that appeals to you. It also doesn't need to live on the floor. The little rug in the photos was made especially to be at home on the seat of a vintage Swedish bench.

One requirement is to choose yarns that are sturdy so the rug will stand up to hard use. Other than that caveat, feel free to use a single color for the rug or put together several colors that match the colorway of the room the rug will be used in. Also, feel free to upcycle T-shirts, old clothing, sheets, or fabric by cutting them into strips and weaving with them.

Equipment

- Dewberry Ridge 6" (15 cm)-wide peg loom or weaving sticks or loom of your choice
- 8 pegs, ⅜" (9 mm) in diameter
- tape measure
- scissors
- warp threader
- blunt tapestry needle
- long glass top pins or T-pins
- large sewing needle and heavy-duty thread
- heavy brown paper
- latch hook

Yarn

- Warp: #4 medium weight acrylic yarn, 3 balls, 1.7 oz./50 g each
- Weft: Country Roving by Briggs & Little (100% pure wool; 8 oz./227 g, 85 yd./78 m), #69 Olive, #01 White, and #41 Navy, 2 balls each

Specs

- WPI: 6 wraps per 1" (2.5 cm)
- Finished Measurements: Approximately 15" (37.5 cm) wide by 45" (112.5 cm) long, or any size or shape that you prefer

Notes

Weaving a circle is a great way to make a swatch to confirm exactly how many pegs will give you the correct dimensions with the warp and weft yarns that you have chosen. You can also check tension, sett, bloom, and draw in.

WEAVING

1. Cut a piece of sturdy brown paper the size that you want the rug to be.

2. Following the instructions on page 35, warp and weave different size circles. Pin them to the paper template.

3. Following the instructions on page 68, warp and weave different size squares. Pin them to the paper template.

4. When you are happy with the placement of the shapes, stitch the shapes together following the instructions on page 26.

5. Make a half hitch cord (see page 24) to go around the outside edges, and stitch it in place.

6. Use the latch hook to pull any ends into the channels of the weaving.

Square Baskets

Baskets are one of the most ancient storage devices invented by humanity. Peg loom and weaving stick versions are very satisfying to weave because they are so useful. They can be a fun way to recycle and upcycle old garments. Baskets are also a great way to showcase art yarns and hand-spun treasure yarns. And, of course, they make practical storage a thing of beauty.

The finished size of the basket is determined by the thickness of the yarn, roving, fabric strips, cords, ribbons, vines, or whatever fiber you choose and also by the diameter of the weaving sticks or pegs.

Equipment

- an odd number of pegs or weaving sticks (The peg loom in the photos is a 6" [15 cm] loom from Dewberry Ridge Looms.)
  - Orange baler twine basket: 7 pegs, ⅜" (9 mm) in diameter
  - Small basket: 7 steel weaving sticks from Daegrad Tools (2 sets of 4 weaving sticks)
  - Medium blue basket: 7 weaving sticks, size small (PLU 262) from Dewberry Ridge Looms (2 sets of 6 weaving sticks)
- tape measure
- scissors
- warp threader
- blunt tapestry needle
- latch hook

Yarn

- Orange baler twine basket:
  - Warp: 1 strand baler twine
  - Weft: 2 strands baler twine
- Small basket:
  - Warp: 1 strand acrylic yarn
  - Weft: 1 strand hand-spun yarn
- Medium blue basket:
  - Warp: 1 strand acrylic yarn
  - Weft: 2 strands hand-spun yarn

Specs

- WPI: Varies according to peg size/spacing and yarn/materials used.
- Finished Measurements:
  - Orange baler twine basket: 11" (27.5 cm) by 11" (27.5 cm) by 11" (27.5 cm)
  - Small basket: 3" (7.5 cm) by 3" (7.5 cm) by 3" (7.5 cm)
  - Medium blue basket: 5" (12.5 cm) by 5" (12.5 cm) by 5" (12.5 cm)

Above: Basket from orange baler twine.

Right: This 5" (12.5 cm) square basket is perfect for holding snippets of yarn and fabric.

Above: Small baskets can highlight hand-spun yarn and fun embellishments.

Notes

- Use a very thick weft to create a dense, firm basket.
- Always weave the squares for the basket on an uneven number of pegs or weaving sticks.
- If you add another square, to form a lid, the basket becomes a box. If you stuff the box and sew the top on permanently, it's a ball or bean bag.

WEAVING

Weave 5 squares, following the directions on page 68. Stitch the 5 squares together (see page 26) with 1 square at the center and the other 4 squares stitched to its edges. Fold the squares up and stitch the corner edges together.

FINISHING

Weave in all ends.

Leaves and Petals

The woven leaf—or petal—shape is a versatile motif that opens up all kinds of design possibilities. It is woven with only three weaving sticks, and is an ingenious combination of a circle and a square. You'll employ short row techniques (see page 36) to create these fun projects.

Equipment

- Dewberry Ridge 10" (25 cm) weaving sticks, ⅛" (3 mm) or ¼" (6 mm) diameter
- tape measure
- scissors
- warp threader
- blunt tapestry or darning needle
- latch hook

Yarn

- Warp: #4 medium weight acrylic yarn, 1 or 2 balls, 1.7 oz./50 g each
- Weft: Country Roving by Briggs & Little (100% pure wool; 8 oz./227 g, 85 yd./78 m), #69 Olive, 1 ball

Specs

- WPI: 6 wraps per 1" (2.5 cm)

Notes

The thickness of the weaving sticks/pegs and the yarn will determine the finished size of the leaf or petal. Also, the number of strands of warp and weft will change the thickness and size of the leaf or petal. If the weft is too thin to make a firm motif, weave with two or more strands held together.

SETUP

Warp strands: Cut 1 or more strands of warp yarn for each weaving stick. When working several of the leaves or petals, instead of measuring warp strands for each motif, cut several warp strands that are at least 2 yd (2 m) long. You will be able to weave several leaves or petals on the same lengths of warp strands, snipping them off after you have tied off the final knots. The warp strands will get shorter, so move the shortest warp strands to the right-hand side as it has the shortest distance to go in each motif.

If you prefer to measure warp for each motif, follow these instructions:

1. Left-hand weaving stick (the outside edge of the leaf): 15" (37.5 cm) working length. The cut length is 30" (75 cm).

2. Middle weaving stick: 12" (30 cm) working length. The cut length is 24" (60 cm).

3. Right-hand weaving stick (the center of the leaf or petal): 8" (20 cm) working length. The cut length is 16" (40 cm).

WEAVING

The leaf or petal is woven by starting at the round base.

1. Beginning at the left side, leave a 6" (15 cm) tail of weft at the base of the first weaving stick.

2. Make a half hitch loop (see page 9) with the tail end of the weft yarn and place it on the first weaving stick.

3. Weave 2 rows on all 3 weaving sticks.

4. Weave 2 rows on 2 weaving sticks.

5. Wrap the left-hand weaving stick twice.

6. Repeat steps 3–5 four more times.

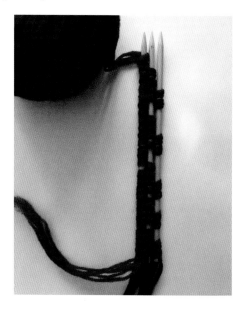

7. Now, weave the pointed half of the motif:
Weave 5 rows on 3 weaving sticks.
Weave 5 rows on 2 weaving sticks.
Wrap the left-hand weaving stick five times.
Weave 5 rows on 2 weaving sticks.
Weave 5 rows on 3 weaving sticks.

8. Break the weft yarn or cut it, leaving a 6" (15 cm) tail.

FINISHING

1. Ease the weaving sticks through the weaving.

2. Pull up the center warp strands firmly to close the center of the motif.

3. Tie a square knot (see page 10), pulling up on the warp strands to close the ring at the center of the leaf or petal.

4. Snip the warp strands about 1" (2.5 cm) from the knot and set the weaving stick aside.

5. Pull up the warp strands on the second weaving stick, leaving about 2" (5 cm) to tie the knot.

6. Tie a square knot with the warp strands and the warp ends, pulling up to draw the beginning and end of the weaving together.

7. Cut the warp strands, leaving a tail of about 1" (2.5 cm).

8. Finish the outside channel of weaving in the same way, drawing the ends of the weaving together and firming up the shape of the motif.

9. Tweak the point of the petal or leaf to clearly define it.

10. If warp strands are showing, stitch over them with the weft tails to cover the knots and gaps.

11. Pull the ends of the warp into each channel with a latch hook or take them into the channels with a tapestry or darning needle.

12. Trim the warp ends flush to the weaving and stroke them with the tip of the weaving stick to make them vanish inside the weaving.

Tip If you are appliquéing the leaf or petal to a background, then don't bother to weave in the warp strands on the back of the motif.

Fanciful Folkloric Flower

The Fanciful Folkloric Flower is woven on only three weaving sticks or the pegs from a peg loom held in your hand as weaving sticks. The Fanciful Folkloric Flower can be used as a motif on rugs, pillows, bags, shawls, or vests. Weave it with wool or other heat-resistant yarn to create a delightful hot pad or trivet.

The petals, center, and leaves are woven separately and then stitched together to form the flower. Because the parts of the flower are woven in small pieces, they are very portable and can be popped into a bag, taken with you, and woven on the go. When the Fanciful Folkloric Flower is woven on ⅛" (3 mm) or ³⁄₃₂" (2.4 mm)-diameter weaving sticks, it can be made into a brooch or used as embellishment on fashion or home décor projects, in scrapbooking, or in card making.

Equipment

- weaving sticks: ¼" (6 mm)-diameter weaving sticks of your choice
- tape measure
- scissors
- warp threader
- blunt tapestry needle
- latch hook
- optional: steam iron

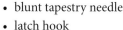
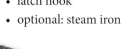

Yarn

- Warp: #4 medium weight acrylic yarn, 3 balls, 1.7 oz./50 g each; 2 strands of yarn held together for the warp
- Weft: Country Roving by Briggs & Little (100% pure wool; 8 oz./227 g, 85 yd./78 m), #69 Olive, #73 Red, and #39 Mustard, 1 ball each

Specs

- WPI: 6 wraps per 1" (2.5 cm)
- Finished Measurements: The finished size of the flower is determined by the thickness of the yarn and diameter of the weaving sticks.

WEAVING

For step-by-step weaving instructions, see Leaves and Petals on page 78.

1. With red yarn (or your choice of color), weave 5 petals for each flower.

2. With yellow yarn (or your choice of color), weave 1 single peg half hitch circle (see page 9) for the center of the flower.

3. With green yarn (or your choice of color), weave as many leaves for each flower as you like.

4. One by one, stitch the points of the petals to the center of the flower. Then stitch about 1" (2.5 cm) of each petal to the petal beside it.

5. Stitch the round edges of the leaves into the spaces between the outside edges of the petals.

6. Use the latch hook to pull any ends into the channels of the weaving or weave in the ends with a tapestry needle.

7. Optional: Lightly steam the flower motif with a steam iron. Hold the iron ½" (1 cm) above the surface of the weaving and push the steam button. Do not rest the iron on the weaving.

Folkloric Flower Pin or Hair Clip

The Folkloric Flower Pin is approximately 3" (7.5 cm) in diameter. From leaf tip to leaf tip is approximately 4" (10 cm). Follow the instructions for the Fanciful Folkloric Flower on page 81, with the following changes:

- Use ⅛" (3 mm)-diameter weaving sticks from Daegrad Tools.
- The warp is 2 strands of crochet cotton and the weft is 2 strands of embroidery floss held together.
- Weave the petals with 2 skeins of cotton embroidery floss (I used floss that was dyed yellow, red, and blue). The leaves take 1 skein of green and the center of the flower takes less than 1 skein of yellow embroidery floss.
- Glue the petals together and then glue the center on. Glue the leaves to the back.
- Glue a circle of felt to the back, and then glue a square of felt and attach a safety pin. An alternate choice is to attach a hair clip to the back.

Folkloric Flowers Rug

The Folkloric Flowers Rug can be woven any size. Because the petals, leaves, and stems are woven in small pieces, they are very portable and can be woven on weaving sticks. Just pop them into a bag, take them with you, and weave on the go.

The finished rug doesn't have to go on the floor. The rug in the photos was woven for the seat of an antique reclaimed and repurposed elders' bench from a church that closed. The original pattern also fit on our vintage Swedish bench—even though it's a touch large.

Equipment

- 12" (30 cm)-wide peg loom (I used Daisy Hill Handiworks model PL120 with ¼" [6 mm] pegs set at ½" [1.25 cm] on center.) or weaving sticks or peg loom in your preferred size
- tape measure
- scissors
- warp threader
- blunt tapestry needle
- long glass top pins or T-pins
- large sewing needle and heavy-duty thread
- heavy brown paper
- latch hook

Yarn

- Warp: #4 medium weight acrylic yarn, 3 balls, 1.7 oz./50 g each; use 2 strands of yarn held together for the warp
- Weft: Country Roving by Briggs & Little (100% pure wool; 8 oz./227 g, 85 yd./78 m), #51 Country Blue, 2 balls; #69 Olive, #73 Red, #39 Mustard, and #41 Navy, 1 ball each

Specs

- WPI: 6 wraps per 1" (2.5 cm)
- Finished Measurements: Approximately 16" (40 cm) wide by 60" (150 cm) long, or any size or shape that you prefer

Notes

- The center panel of the background is woven first. Then the border panels are woven separately and stitched to the center panel. The flowers, leaves, and stems are also woven separately and later appliquéd to the background.
- Weave a gauge swatch to check your measurements, especially if you are working with a different size loom than listed in the directions.

SETUP

The working length of warp for the background panel and border sections is 72" (1.8 m). The cut length is 144" (3.7 m).

WEAVING

1. Warp the center panel with 2 strands held together. With light blue, weave the center panel on 24 pegs.

2. With navy, weave the border edgings on 4 pegs. Use 2 strands of yarn held together for the warp.

3. Weave 4 flowers following the instructions on page 78. Warp and weave 5 petals for each flower. Weave 1 single peg circle (see page 35) for each flower. Stitch each flower together.

4. Warp and weave as many leaves as you would like following the instructions on page 78. Pin them to the flowers and stitch them in place.

5. Use the latch hook to pull any ends into the channels of the weaving.

FINISHING

1. Finish the ends of the center panel with an edging of double Damascus knots (see page 17).

2. Finish the starting edge of the border panels with double Damascus knots, but not the last edge.

3. Adjust the length of the border panels to match the center panel and pin them together.

4. Stitch the border sections to the center panels.

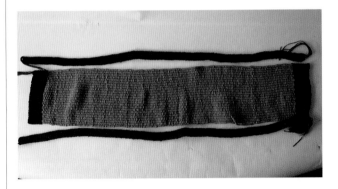

5. Work the double Damascus knots along the final edges of the 2 side panels.

6. Pin the flowers to the background and stitch them in place.

Circles on a Square Heart

Woven hearts make nice 3-D elements for cards and scrapbooking.

how your love with a sweet little woven heart. Stitch on jewelry findings and it becomes a hair clip, necklace, or brooch. Appliqué these hearts to baskets, bags, prayer shawls, buntings, scarves, pillows, hats, rugs, or vests. Or glue them to cards and scrapbook pages. They can even be used as doll wings. The mask on page 169 was embellished with several of these woven hearts.

The Circles on a Square Heart is formed when 2 circles mash up with a square. Each heart takes very little yarn, so you can use up scraps or use the heart motif to sample special hand-spun or art yarns. Weaving a heart is also an excellent way to swatch for larger projects, as you will learn so much about the way the yarn you have chosen will work with your weaving sticks or peg loom—with the bonus of having a heart, too.

Equipment

- Dewberry Ridge 10" (25 cm) weaving sticks, ⅜" (9 mm) or ¼" (6 mm) diameter, or weaving sticks of your choice
- tape measure
- scissors
- warp threader
- blunt tapestry needle
- latch hook

Yarn

- Warp: #4 medium weight acrylic yarn, 1 or 2 balls, 1.7 oz./50 g each
- Weft: Handspun by Nomad Fibreworks (99% wool, 1% Firestar); Atlantic by Briggs & Little (100% pure wool; 4 oz./113 g, 135 yd./123 m), #30 Fern Green, 1 ball; Super by Briggs & Little (100% pure wool; 4 oz./113 g, 85 yd./77 m), #30 Fern Green, 1 ball (use 1 strand)

Specs

- WPI: Handspun, 8 wraps per 1" (2.5 cm); Atlantic, 8 wraps per 1" (2.5 cm); Super, 6 wraps per 1" (2.5 cm)
- Finished Measurements: Approximately 1" (2.5 cm) to 2¾" (7 cm) tall

Notes

- The heart is woven with 3 weaving sticks, ¼" (6 mm) diameter. There are no knots securing the ends. Simply weave the ends in to finish the heart and complete the shaping.
- The finished size of the heart is determined by the size of weaving sticks that you use as well as the thickness of the warp strands and weft yarn.
- The weaving needs to be quite dense, so use fairly thick yarn. If the weft is too thin to make a firm motif, use multiple strands held together. You can also use roving, fabric strips, or T-shirt yarn for weft.

SETUP

Warp strands: Cut 1 or more strands of warp yarn for each weaving stick:

- For a medium-size heart, about 6" (15 cm) across, the working length is 30" (75 cm) on ¼" (6 mm) weaving sticks.
- For smaller hearts on thinner weaving sticks, use less warp.
- For larger hearts with thicker yarn and bigger weaving sticks, use slightly longer warp.

Left to right: hearts worked in Super, Atlantic, and Handspun.

WEAVING

1. Starting at the first upper "shoulder" of the heart and beginning at the left side, leave a 6" (15 cm) tail of weft at the base of the first weaving stick.

2. Make a half hitch loop (see page 9) with the tail end of the weft yarn and place it on the first weaving stick at the left-hand edge.

3. Wrap the left-hand weaving stick four times more after the half hitch.

    Weave 2 rows on 3 weaving sticks.

    Weave 2 rows on 2 weaving sticks.

    Wrap the left-hand weaving stick once.

    Repeat step 3 one more time.

4. Weave the first half of the lower part of the heart:

    Weave 4 rows on 3 weaving sticks.

    Weave 4 rows on 2 weaving sticks.

    Wrap the left-hand weaving stick seven times for the point of the heart.

5. Weave the other half of the lower part of the heart:
Weave 4 rows on 2 weaving sticks.
Weave 4 rows on all 3 weaving sticks.

6. Weave the second upper "shoulder" of the heart:
Wrap the left-hand weaving stick once.
Weave 2 rows on 2 weaving sticks.
Weave 2 rows on 3 weaving sticks.
Repeat this step one more time.

7. Wrap the left-hand weaving stick four times.

8. End with a half hitch knot on the left-hand edge weaving stick.

9. Break or cut the weft yarn, leaving a 6" (15 cm) tail for finishing.

FINISHING

1. Ease the weaving sticks through the weaving.

2. Cut the warp strands, leaving tails of about 3" (7.5 cm) on each channel, at both ends of the weaving. *Note:* For a larger heart, cut the warp strands longer; for a small heart, cut them shorter.

3. Ease the tails out of the half hitches at the outside ends of the weaving, leaving 5 wraps at each end.

4. Form a V shape by holding both ends of the center channel and pulling up on them. At the same time, pull down on the point of the V.

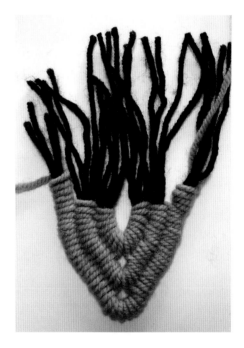

5. On the first shoulder of the heart, insert the tapestry or craft needle into the second channel, bringing the needle out close to the point.

6. Thread the warp ends from the center channel into the needle and pull them through the channel, leaving the ends for now.

7. Insert the tapestry or craft needle into the outside channel, bringing the needle out close to the point.

8. Thread the warp ends from the second channel into the needle and pull them through the channel, leaving the ends for now.

9. Insert the tapestry or craft needle into the center channel, bringing the needle out close to the point.

10. Thread the warp ends from the outside channel into the needle and pull them through the channel, leaving the ends for now.

11. Repeat this process for the other shoulder.

12. Gently tug on the warp ends to shape the heart and to close any gaps in the weaving.

13. After the warp ends from the outside channel have been taken through the center channels, tie a half knot (take one set of ends over and under the other set of strands) and then pull up.

14. Take the ends up through the outside channel to secure them.

15. Trim the warp ends flush with the heart.

16. Thread the weft ends into the tapestry needle and stitch over any gaps.

17. Use the tip of the needle to stroke the weft strands into place if needed.

18. Weave in the weft ends.

The woven hearts make lovely brooches or hair clips. Stitch or glue whichever closure you prefer to the back. Embellish the finished hearts with beads, buttons, charms, or whatever takes your fancy.

CHAPTER 6

Dolls and Toys

One of the greatest pleasures in being a weaver is the delight in making unique gifts for family and friends. You might not think of weaving toys on these simple looms, but let's look at what we can do with a little creativity and ingenuity.

"Nreenie" dolls are small flat dolls I designed for weaving on peg looms or weaving sticks. "Pegagurumi" toys are my homage to the knitted and crocheted amigurumi beloved by yarn aficionados. As you will see, Nreenie dolls and pegagurumi toys are small and easy to make, and offer endless opportunities for creating one-of-a-kind treasures.

I hope you will love weaving them and that your family and friends will enjoy receiving them!

Nreenie Dolls

When I first began weaving with weaving sticks and peg looms almost two decades ago, my first projects were small woven dolls. This was not a surprise, as I have been a doll maker all my life, and I have always loved the smallest dolls the most. I have designed many, many dolls to weave on the peg loom or with weaving sticks over the years. I love trying to see how simple I can make a design but still have it clearly be a celebration of the human form. Nreenie dolls are woven with only three weaving sticks. Simple, yes, but still conveying essence.

Nreenie dolls can easily be made in different sizes by using larger or smaller weaving sticks or pegs. The creative possibilities are completely unlimited; each doll will be unique because of the face that you make or find for her, the yarns that you choose, whether you weave patterns in her body or embellish her. Nreenie dolls are a good way to upcycle old clothing instead of throwing it away. Now, a favorite worn-out garment can be cut into strips for a Nreenie doll and live on in a new way.

Nreenie dolls can be hung up as ornaments if you attach a hanger to the head. The smaller ones can be worn as a necklace or pin if you attach jewelry findings to them.

Equipment

- 3 weaving sticks or pegs
- warp threader
- scissors
- ruler or tape measure
- craft needle
- needle and thread to sew on buttons and embellishments
- hot glue gun or thick craft glue
- punches for circles or ovals and hearts
- latch hook
- felting needle (optional)

Yarn

- Warp: Use yarns, strings, or thread that fit the size of your weaving sticks. The warp strands can be used to make the hair or you can add other choices for hair.
- Weft: Use whatever string, cords, ribbons, lace, yarn, roving, or thread that appeals to you. Hand-spun and art yarns are great, and so are T-shirt yarns and fabric strips torn from worn-out clothing. Combine multiple strands of crochet cotton or sewing machine threads and use them as if they're a single strand. The plastic tape that is sold for packing and moving (without adhesive on it) weaves up really well after it has served its purpose during the move.
- Embellishments: Use heart-shaped buttons, beads, or stickers or a paper-punched heart for the chest. Use a butterfly punch for wings for small Nreenie dolls and a permanent ink fine-tip marker or pencil crayons to draw details. Other embellishments include self-cover buttons and fabric for faces, beads, buttons, charms, acorn caps, found objects, wooden circles or ovals, sequins, lace, and bottle caps.

Specs

- Finished Measurements:
  - ⅛" (3 mm)-diameter weaving sticks make a Nreenie doll that is approximately 2" (5 cm) tall.
  - ¼" (6 mm)-diameter weaving sticks make a Nreenie doll that is approximately 5" (12.5 cm) tall.
  - ⅜" (9 mm)-diameter weaving sticks make a Nreenie doll that is approximately 6" (15 cm) tall.
  - ½" (1.25 cm)-diameter weaving sticks make a Nreenie doll that is approximately 7½" (18.75 cm) tall.

Dolls woven on weaving sticks that are ⅛" (3 mm) in diameter.

These dolls were woven on a variety of types of looms and weaving sticks, but the pegs were all ¼" (6 mm) in diameter, yielding a doll approximately 5" (12.5 cm) tall.

Dolls woven on weaving sticks that are ⅜" (9 mm) in diameter. Dolls are small and perfect for experimenting with a variety of materials, such as fabric strips and nonadhesive wrap tape. Buttons and tiny toys add charm.

This doll was woven on ½" (1.25 cm)-diameter weaving sticks and is approximately 7½" (18.75 cm) tall.

WEAVING

You may choose to weave with more than 1 color of weft yarn and add patterns to the body. See page 131 for instructions on how to weave geometric patterns.

1. Warp 3 pegs or weaving sticks with warp strands with a working length as follows:
- ⅛" (3 mm)-diameter weaving sticks: 10" (25 cm) long. The cut length is 20" (50 cm).
- ¼" (6 mm)-diameter weaving sticks: 13" (32.5 cm) long. The cut length is 26" (65 cm).
- ⅜" (9 mm)- and ½" (1.25 cm)-diameter weaving sticks: 16" (40 cm) long. The cut length is 32" (80 cm).

2. Weave the body length as below, leaving about a 10" (25 cm) tail of weft for finishing.

- On ⅛" (3 mm)-diameter weaving sticks: 2" (5 cm)
- On ¼" (6 mm)-diameter weaving sticks: 3½" (8.75 cm)
- On ⅜" (9 mm)- and ½" (1.25 cm)-diameter weaving sticks: 4" (10 cm)
- On ½" (1.25 cm)-diameter weaving sticks: 5" (12.5 cm)

3. Advance the warp on the middle peg by sliding it up the distance listed below. This will act as a guide in making the arms, as it sets the height of the top of the head.
- On ⅛" (3 mm)-diameter weaving sticks: ¾" (1.9 cm)
- On ¼" (6 mm)-diameter weaving sticks: 1½" (3.8 cm)
- On ⅜" (9 mm)- and ½" (1.25 cm)-diameter weaving sticks: 2" (5 cm)

4. Make the arms with the same color yarn as the body or with a different color. Slide the side pegs out so there is approximately 2"–3" (5–7.5 cm) of warp at the lower edge of the weaving.

5. Take the right-hand weaving stick over the center peg in an arch and then lay it alongside the left-hand side of the weaving. Take the left-hand weaving stick over the center peg in an arch and then lay it alongside the right-hand side of the weaving, laying these warp strands on top of the first ones.

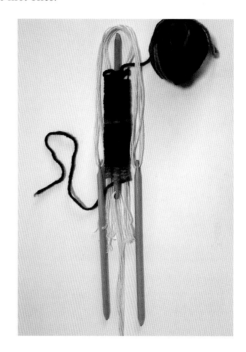

6. Cut 1 to 2 yd. (.9 to 1.8 m) of weft yarn and thread the end into a craft needle. Take the yarn through the needle until the needle is almost at the center, leaving a 6" (15 cm) tail for finishing.

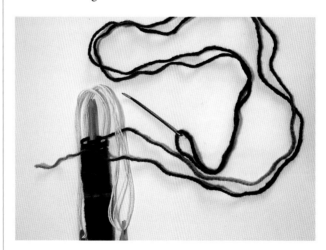

7. Using the needle, wrap the loops closely and firmly to shape the arms.

8. Complete the arms by making 2 half hitch knots on the center weaving stick.

9. Turn the side weaving sticks so they are pointing upward and place them on both sides of the center weaving stick. Note that loops of warp still hang from the 2 side weaving sticks. They will be pulled up later.

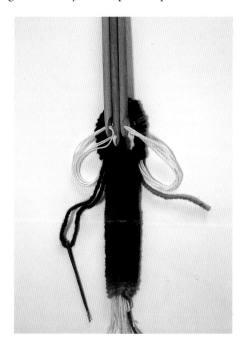

10. Weave the head with the same color as the body or with a different color. Join the ball of yarn, leaving a 4" (10 cm) tail for finishing, and weave:
- On ⅛" (3 mm)-diameter weaving sticks: ¾" (1.9 cm)
- On ¼" (6 mm)-diameter weaving sticks: 1" (2.5 cm)
- On ⅜" (9 mm)- and ½" (1.3 cm)-diameter weaving sticks: 1½" (3.8 cm)

11. Snip the weft yarn from the ball, leaving a 4" (10 cm) tail.

12. Ease the weaving sticks all the way out of the head so the head meets the body and all the warp ends at the hem are the same length and the loops hanging from the arms are pulled through, leaving no gaps.

13. Trim the center warp strands so they are the same length as the outside ones.

14. Divide the warp strands in half.

15. Take one set over and under the other set.

16. Pull up gently to close the top of the head.

17. Weave the warp ends down through the outside channels of the head using a latch hook.

18. Weave them through the half hitches at the neck.

19. Weave in the ends.

20. To shape the neck, wrap the tail end strands of weft yarn from the arms and head around the neck area several times. Weave the yarn ends into the head.

21. Use the remaining yarn in the needle to cover any gaps in the warp at the shoulders. Weave the ends into the body and snip the needle from the yarn.

22. Use the needle to stitch over the top of the head with the weft yarn tail end, and then weave the end into the head.

23. Use the same finishing process as the top of the head to clean finish the hem.

FINISHING

Hair

If you want to use the warp ends as hair, don't do a clean finish. Instead, make a tassel with the warp ends. If the warp strands don't make a generous enough head of hair, feel free to add more strands by knotting or gluing them in place. Roving or fleece can also be used to enhance the hair. You can use the warp strands or other bits of yarn or fleece to twist, snip, loop, braid, or make bangs for the Nreenie doll.

If you do use the clean finish for the top of the head, you can stitch or glue on yarn, fleece, fabric strips, or roving as hair and/or add a hat.

The warp ends can be made into a tassel for hair.

Roving or fleece can be glued or stitched on for hair.

Face

There are many different ways to make a face. Here are a few to try:

Cut out a circle or oval of card stock, draw a face on it, then glue it to the head.

Glue or stitch a button to the head.

Make a wooden face from a slice of a twig or a purchased wooden oval or circle

Use a charm for the face.

Cover a button with cloth and paint or draw a face, then stitch or glue it to the head

Wings

There are a few different options for making wings, if desired.

Weave them, making either 2 leaf shapes (see page 78) or 2 hearts (see page 86).

Use a punch to make a butterfly from card stock, and glue it in place as wings.

If the Nreenie doll is too large for a single butterfly to work, punch out 2 and fold them in half. Glue the folded sides of the butterfly together and then glue to the back of the doll.

Cut wings out of metal foil and stitch or glue them on.

Use lace or embroidered butterflies from the notions section of your local fabric or craft store.

Heart

Nreenie dolls must have a heart, so add a heart button or bead, or punch one out of card stock. Embellish the Nreenie doll in any way that appeals to you: lace for shawls, found objects, beads, buttons, charms, shells, acorn caps, and broken jewelry are just a few ideas.

Nreenie doll woven on Clover Weaving Sticks using recycled sari silk yarn.

Nreenie doll woven on ⅛″ (3 mm)-diameter pegs by Daegrad Tools using embroidery floss.

Nreenie doll woven on ¼″ (6 mm)-diameter pegs by Lee Valley using Lion Brand yarn.

Nreenie doll woven on ⅜" (9 mm)-diameter pegs by Dewberry Ridge using upcycled cling packing tape. (This tape doesn't have the sticky goo on it, so it acts like yarn when it's taken off whatever it was holding in place during a move.)

Nreenie doll woven on ½" (1.3 cm)-diameter pegs by Dewberry Ridge using roving from Briggs & Little.

Nreenie doll woven on ⅜" (9 mm)-diameter pegs by Dewberry Ridge using fabric strips.

Nreenie doll woven on ¼" (6 mm)-diameter pegs by Lee Valley using hand-spun yarn by Nomad Fibreworks.

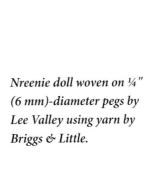

Nreenie doll woven on ¼" (6 mm)-diameter pegs by Daisy Hill Handiworks using hand-spun yarn by Nomad Fibreworks.

Nreenie doll woven on ¼" (6 mm)-diameter pegs by Lee Valley using yarn by Briggs & Little.

Pegagurumi Woven Toys

egagurumi woven toys are adorable little toys woven on weaving sticks. Pegagurumi are a wonderful way to use small amounts of yarn, and the variations are endless. The basic body of the pegagurumi is a ball-shaped head, a cone-shaped body that has a circular base, and half hitch spirals for arms and legs. The basic body is used in all the pegagurumi, but the ears, noses, tails, and other details are changed to make each of the pegagurumi woven toys unique.

Equipment

- 6 weaving sticks ¼" (6 mm) in diameter and 10" (25 cm) long
- warp threader
- scissors
- tape measure or ruler
- felting needle (optional)
- stuffing—either polyester stuffing or snipped up yarn for stuffing
- black beads or buttons ¼" (6 mm) in diameter, for eyes
- embroidery floss or yarn to embroider eyes, mouths, and noses

Yarn

- Warp: 2 strands of #4 medium weight worsted acrylic yarn of any color
- Weft: Atlantic by Briggs & Little (100% pure wool; 4 oz./113 g, 135 yd./123 m), 1 ball of each color needed for the project

Specs

- WPI: 7 wraps per 1" (2.5 cm)
- Finished Measurements: Approximately 3½" (8.75 cm) tall

Notes

- The instructions are for ¼" (6 mm)-diameter weaving sticks, as weaving sticks held together can create a more dense fabric than peg looms, which have spaces between the pegs.
- If you prefer to use smaller weaving sticks, your pegagurumi will be smaller and your working warp length can be shorter. If you choose to use thicker weaving sticks, the pegagurumi will be larger and the working length of the warp length will need to be longer.
- If you use thinner yarn, you may need to use 2 strands held together to achieve the results in the patterns.
- If you prefer to use a peg loom rather than weaving sticks, feel free. The pegagurumi may be somewhat larger because of the set of the peg loom.
- **Important:** If you are going to give the pegagurumi to young children, *do not* use beads or buttons for embellishments. They present a choking hazard.

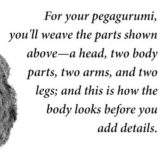

For your pegagurumi, you'll weave the parts shown above—a head, two body parts, two arms, and two legs; and this is how the body looks before you add details.

Pegagurumi Arms and Legs

The arms and legs are made with half hitch spirals on a single weaving stick. You'll make four total. The spirals are a closely packed series of half hitch knots that slide and twist into a spiral along warp strands. A lock knot at the end prevents the half hitches from escaping.

One end is completely finished, with no warp ends hanging from it. That's because the warp yarn is also the weft yarn, used to make the half hitch knots. When the yarn end is pulled through the half hitches, it has to be secured. The lock knot keeps the half hitch spiral secure by providing an anchor for the half hitch knots.

WEAVING

1. About 3" (7.5 cm) from the end of the warp strands, tie a lock knot by making a loop and taking the end of the yarn through the loop three times. Ease the 3 wraps together before pulling up firmly to close the lock knot.

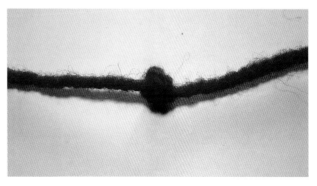

2. Thread the yarn end through the hole in the weaving stick and pull the lock knot up against the weaving stick.

3. With the same strand of yarn, start making the half hitches on the weaving stick:

Hold the weaving stick in your nondominant hand and take the yarn over the index finger of your dominant hand, forming a loop like the letter *e*.

Insert the weaving stick into the loop, lift it off your finger, then lightly pull on the yarn to slide it gently down the weaving stick until it rests against the lock knot.

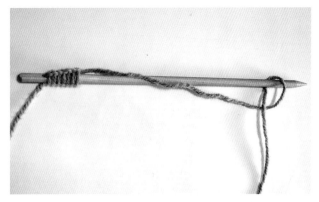

Repeat these steps 17 times, packing the half hitches closely together and twisting them into a spiral.

Cut the yarn from the ball, leaving a 3" (7.5 cm) tail.

4. Pull the tail of the warp strand back through the hole in the weaving stick, leaving a tail end of about ½" (1.3 cm) on one side of the hole and a loop between the knot and other side of the hole of the weaving stick. This allows the weaving stick to move through the half hitch knots. Advance the spiral onto the warp strands by sliding the weaving stick up through the half hitches.

5. Ease the half hitches along the warp strands until the weaving stick comes all the way through the spiral.

FINISHING

1. Pull up firmly on the warp strand that comes up from the center of the spiral until the spiral is firm and solid, and about 1" (2.5 cm) long.

2. Pull up hard on the weft yarn end (the yarn that came off the ball). This locks the spiral in place.

3. Tie the ends together firmly in a square knot (see page 10). The yarn ends will be used to sew the spiral to the pegagurumi.

Pegagurumi Basic Body

Body Base

Make the body base by weaving 1 circle on 3 weaving sticks.

SETUP

1. Warp the left-hand weaving stick (the outside edge weaving stick) with 2 strands of #4 medium weight worsted yarn held together for a working length of 16" (40 cm). The cut length is 32" (80 cm).

2. Warp the center weaving stick with 2 strands of #4 medium weight worsted yarn held together for a working length of 10" (25 cm). The cut length is 20" (50 cm).

3. Warp the right-hand weaving stick with 2 strands of #4 medium weight worsted yarn held together for a working length of 6" (15 cm). The cut length is 12" (30 cm).

WEAVING

1. Beginning at the left side (which will be the outside edge of the circle), leave a 5" (12.5 cm) tail of weft.

2. Make a half hitch loop with the tail end of the weft yarn and place it on the first weaving stick.

3. Weave 2 rows on all 3 weaving sticks.
Weave 2 rows on 2 weaving sticks.
Wrap the left weaving stick once.

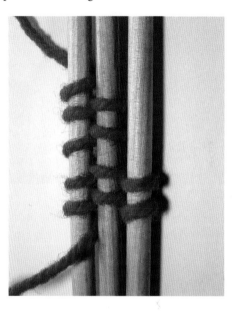

4. Repeat step 3, weaving the circle and advancing the weft when needed until you have 6" (15 cm) of weft on the left-hand outside edge weaving stick. This will be the circumference of the circle.

5. End the weaving by making a half hitch knot on the last weaving stick. Snip the weft end.

FINISHING

1. Ease the warp strands through the weft until the circle lies flat and the warp ends at the end of the beginning of the circle are about 3" (7.5 cm) long.

2. Tie firm square knots in the warp ends, matching each channel carefully to secure them.

3. Cut the warp yarns from the weaving sticks, leaving about 2" (5 cm) for each tail at the knots.

4. The yarn ends do not need to be woven in, as they will be inside the body.

Body Cone

Weave 1 cone to make the body.

SETUP

1. Warp 4 weaving sticks with 2 strands of #4 medium weight worsted yarn held together for a working length of 16" (40 cm). The cut length is 32" (80 cm).

2. The center weaving stick of the cone is placed at the right side and the rest of the weaving sticks are placed to the left of it, ending with the weaving stick that will be the outside lower edge of the cone at the left-hand side.

WEAVING

The cone is woven using the short row technique:

1. Beginning at the left side, leave a 6" (15 cm) tail of weft.

2. Make a half hitch knot with the tail end of the weft yarn, twist it once, and place it on the first weaving stick.

3. Weave 3 rows on all 4 weaving sticks.
   Weave 3 rows on 3 weaving sticks.
   Weave 3 rows on 2 weaving sticks.
   Wrap the left-hand edge weaving stick once.

4. Repeat step 3, advancing the weft when needed, until the weaving is 6" (15 cm) on the left-hand weaving stick. Weave lots of rows to make the weaving very dense.

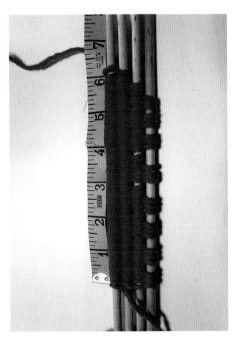

5. Make a half hitch knot on the last weaving stick. Snip the weft end, leaving a 3" (7.5 cm) tail.

FINISHING

1. Ease the warp strands through the weaving until the warp ends at the end of each channel are close to the same length.

2. Tie knots in the warp ends to secure them. Cut the warp yarns from the weaving sticks. Take the yarn ends inside the cone.

3. Stuff the cone firmly.

4. Stitch the base to the cone.

Pegagurumi Head

Weave 1 ball for the head.

SETUP

Warp 6 weaving sticks with 2 strands of #4 medium weight worsted yarn held together for a working length of 16" (40 cm). The cut length is 32" (80 cm).

WEAVING

Weave the ball using a short row technique that alternates skipping the edge weaving sticks.

1. Beginning at the left side, leave a 6" (15 cm) tail of weft.

2. Make a half hitch knot with the tail end of the weft yarn, twist it once, and place it on the first weaving stick. (The yarn end will be woven in after the weaving is complete.)

3. Weave across all 6 weaving sticks, from left to right.

Weave from the right across 5 weaving sticks, skipping the edge weaving stick on the left-hand side.

Weave 4 weaving sticks from the left to the right-hand side, skipping the edge weaving stick on the right side.

Weave 5 weaving sticks from the right to left all the way to the edge weaving stick at the left-hand side.

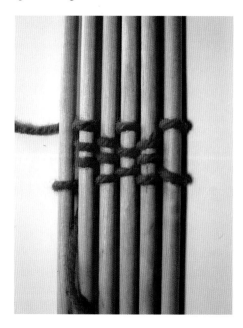

4. Repeat step 3, weaving very densely, with the weft packed firmly and advancing the weft when needed, until the weaving on the center pegs measures 6" (15 cm).

5. End the weaving by making a half hitch knot on the last weaving stick. Snip the weft end.

FINISHING

1. Cut the warp yarns at the weaving sticks.

2. Ease the warp strands through the weaving until the warp ends at the end of each channel are close to the same length.

3. Pull up the warp strands on one edge of the weaving sticks, snip the weaving stick off, and pull up the warp ends tightly. Tie knots in the warp ends to secure them.

4. Repeat on the other side of the weaving. Tuck the warp ends from the centers of the ball inside the ball.

5. Stuff the ball firmly. Snip the remaining weaving sticks off, one at a time, and tie knots to secure the ends. Push the warp ends inside the ball with one of the weaving sticks or a pencil, then smooth out any lumps or bumps and arrange the weft to cover the knots. If necessary, use the weft ends from the beginning and end of the weaving to stitch over any knots that still show. Squish and squeeze the ball into a pleasing shape. Use a felting needle to secure any odds and ends of yarn that need to be worked into place.

Final Steps

1. Stitch the head to the body.

2. Stitch arms to the shoulder area and legs to the hips.

3. Weave in the ends.

Elephant

Yarn

- Weft: Atlantic by Briggs & Little (100% pure wool; 4 oz./113 g, 135 yd./123 m), Medium Grey, 1 ball

Additional Materials

- 2 black beads ¼" (6 mm) in diameter or black embroidery floss, for eyes
- yarn or embroidery floss for nose and mouth
- stuffing

Body, Arms, Legs, and Head

Weave the Pegagurumi Basic Body, Arms and Legs, and Head (see pages 108–112) with 1 strand of yarn, and stitch them together.

Ears (Make 2)

The ear is a small square made with 3 weaving sticks. The finished size of the ear is approximately 2" (5 cm) on each side.

SETUP

1. The working length of the warp strands for the left-hand weaving stick is 12" (30 cm). The cut length is 24" (60 cm). *Note:* The middle warp strand can be shorter and the right-hand weaving stick only needs about 8" (20 cm) working length.

2. Cut 2 strands of warp strands for each of the 3 weaving sticks.

WEAVING

1. With 1 strand of weft, place a half hitch on the first weaving stick on the left-hand side.

2. Wrap the left-hand weaving stick three times.

3. Weave 4 rows on 2 weaving sticks.
Weave 2 rows on 3 weaving sticks.
Weave 4 rows on 2 weaving sticks.
Wrap the left-hand weaving stick three times.

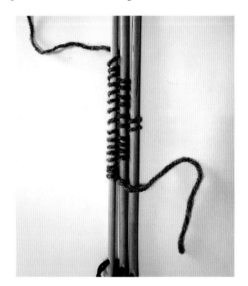

4. Repeat step 3 three more times.

FINISHING

1. Ease the warp strands all the way through the weaving so you have warp strands at the beginning and ending of the weaving.

2. Beginning at the center of the square, pull up on the warp ends and tie square knots with the warp ends to secure them, matching the warp ends carefully. Make sure you are tying the knot in the same channel and not with the neighboring warp strands.

3. As you tie the knots, push on the weft strands with your fingers to move them into a square shape of the desired size.

4. Weave half the warp ends into the channels on one side of the knots; weave the remaining half of the warp strands into the channels on the other side of the knots. At the center, take the ends through the weaving several times to secure them.

5. Use the ends of the weft yarn to stitch the ears to the side of the head.

6. Fold 2 corners of 1 square together and stitch it to the side of the head.

Repeat for the second ear.

Trunk and Tail

1. For the trunk, make 1 half hitch spiral 1½" (3.75 cm) long (see page 108).

2. Stitch the trunk to the face.

3. For the tail, take 2 strands of yarn approximately 6" (15 cm) long through the lower edge of the back of the elephant. Bring the yarn strands out so you have 3" (7.5 cm) on each side of 1 stitch.

4. Twist the yarn strands really hard, then bring them together to twirl around each other.

5. Tie an overhand knot in the ends. Trim the ends.

Final Steps

1. For the eyes: Stitch 2 beads to the face or embroider black eyes.

2. For the mouth: With pink or red embroidery floss or yarn, take 2 short stitches for the mouth. Make 2 tiny stitches over the center of the mouth stitches to secure them.

3. Take all ends inside the head.

Yarn

- Weft: Atlantic by Briggs & Little (100% pure wool; 4 oz./113 g, 135 yd./123 m), #14 Sheep's Grey, 1 ball

Other Materials

- 2 black beads ¼" (6 mm) in diameter or black embroidery floss, for eyes
- yarn or embroidery floss for nose and mouth
- stuffing

Body, Arms, Legs, and Head

Weave the Pegagurumi Basic Body, Arms and Legs, and Head (see page 106) with 1 strand of yarn and stitch them together.

Ears (Make 2)

Weave the ear on 2 weaving sticks. The finished size of the ear is approximately 1½" (3.75 cm) across.

SETUP

Warp both weaving sticks with 2 strands of #4 medium weight worsted yarn held together for a working length of 6" (15 cm). The cut length is 12" (30 cm).

WEAVING

1. Beginning at the left side (which will be the outside edge of the ear), leave a 5" (12.5 cm) tail of weft at the base of the first weaving stick.

2. Make a half hitch loop with the tail end of the weft yarn and place it on the first weaving stick.

3. Wrap the left-hand weaving stick twice. Weave 1 row on both weaving sticks.

4. Repeat step 3, advancing the weft when needed. Continue weaving until you have 3½" (8.75 cm) of weft on the left-hand weaving stick. This will be the outside circumference of the ear.

5. End the weaving by making a half hitch knot on the left-hand weaving stick. Snip the weft end. Slide the weaving sticks through the weaving.

6. For the right-hand weaving stick (center of the ear), tie a square knot with the warp ends. Snip the warp ends to about 3" (7.5 cm) long.

7. For the left-hand weaving stick (outside of the ear), snip the warp strands so they are about 3" (7.5 cm) long. Don't tie a knot with the outside ear ends, as they will be used to stitch the ear to the side of the head.

Repeat for the second ear.

Nose

Use black yarn to make 1 nose.

WEAVING

1. Using 1 weaving stick, make 11 half hitch knots. Ease them down the warp strands. Leave a few inches at the end. Then snip the warp strands a few inches away from the half hitch knots.

2. Pull up on the warp strands and tie a tight square knot to form the ring.

3. Thread the weft end into a darning needle and stitch through the top of the adjacent stitch to close the ring.

4. Trim the warp ends to about ½" (1 cm).

Finishing

1. For the ears: Use the warp strand ends to stitch the ears to the side of the koala's head. Weave the weft ends inside the head.

2. For the nose: Stitch the nose to the middle of the face.

3. For the eyes: Stitch 2 beads to the face or embroider black eyes.

4. For the mouth: With pink or red embroidery floss or yarn, take 2 short stitches for the mouth. Take 2 tiny stitches over the center of the mouth stitches to secure them.

5. Take all ends inside the head.

Panda

Yarn

- Atlantic by Briggs & Little (100% pure wool; 4 oz./113 g, 135 yd./123 m), #02 Washed White and #16 Black, 1 ball each

Other Materials

- 2 black beads ¼" (6 mm) in diameter or black embroidery floss, for eyes
- yarn or embroidery floss for nose and mouth
- stuffing

Body, Arms, Legs, and Head

Weave the Pegagurumi Basic Body and Head (see page 106) with 1 strand of white yarn. Use white warp strands for the white head and body. Stitch them together.

Make 4 Pegagurumi Arms and Legs with black yarn following instructions for the half hitch spirals on page 108. Stitch them to the panda's body.

Eye Patches and Ears

Make 2 eye patches with black yarn following the instructions for the Koala Nose on page 118.

Make 2 ears with black yarn following the instructions for the Koala Ears on page 117.

Finishing

1. For the ears: Use the warp strands to stitch each ear to the panda's head by taking the warp strands inside the head at the base of the ear. Each set goes into the head and comes out at the entry point of the other corner of the ear. Pull on the warp strands to form an arch shape, then bury the warp ends inside the head. Stitch the corners of the ears to the head with the weft ends and take them inside the head.

2. For the nose: Embroider a small black nose to the middle of the face.

3. For the eyes: Stitch the 2 eye patches to the panda's face. Stitch 2 beads to the face or embroider black eyes with contrasting black embroidery floss or glossy yarn.

4. For the mouth: With pink or red embroidery floss or yarn, make 2 short stitches for the mouth. Place 2 tiny stitches over the center of the mouth stitches to secure them.

5. Take all ends inside the head.

Yarn

Atlantic by Briggs & Little (100% pure wool; 4 oz./113 g, 135 yd./123 m), #02 Washed White and #16 Black, 1 ball each

Other Materials

- 2 black beads ¼" (6 mm) in diameter or black embroidery floss, for eyes
- 1 red *e* bead or embroidery floss, for mouth
- 3 black *e* beads or black embroidery floss or yarn, for lumps of coal
- 1 small orange bead or button for nose
- 2 short twigs for arms
- thick craft glue or hot glue gun, if necessary, to secure arms
- stuffing

Body, Head, and Arms

Weave the Pegagurumi Basic Body and Head (see page 106) with 1 strand of white yarn. Use white warp strands for the white head and body. Stitch them together.

Find 2 interesting little twigs and insert them into the snowman for arms; glue them in place if necessary. If you prefer to make half hitch spiral arms, do so with a brown yarn following the instructions on page 108.

Hat

WEAVING

1. For the crown: Make 1 circle with black yarn using 3 pegs. See instructions on page 35.

Tie the 2 center sets of warp strands; pull up the outside strand of warp to shape the circle into a dome shape for the crown.

Tie a square knot to secure the shape.

2. For the brim: Warp: Cut 2 strands of yarn that are a working length of 18" (45 cm). The cut length is 36" (90 cm). Thread them into 2 weaving sticks.

With black yarn: Leave a 3" (7.5 cm) tail of weft and make a half hitch knot on 1 weaving stick.

Weave 2 rows on both weaving sticks.

Wrap the left-hand weaving stick once.

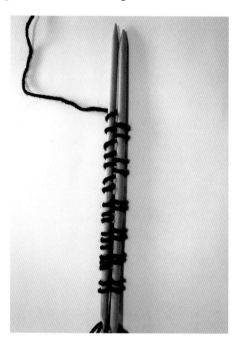

3. Continue weaving 2 rows and wrapping the left-hand stick until the weaving is 12" (30 cm) long and you have 3" (7.5 cm) of warp strands at each end of the weaving.

4. Cut the weft, leaving a 3" (7.5 cm) tail.

5. Pull up on the right-hand weaving stick to gather and shape the brim.

6. Pull up on the warp strands to shape the brim to the crown.

7. Tie square knots to close the brim. Weave the ends into the brim.

8. Stitch the brim to the lower edge of the crown.

Finishing

1. For the hat: Stitch or glue the hat to the snowman's head.

2. For the nose: Embroider a small orange nose to the middle of the face or stitch on a small orange button.

3. For the eyes: Stitch 2 black ¼" (6 mm)-diameter beads to the snowman's face or embroider eyes with black embroidery floss or glossy yarn.

4. For the mouth: With pink or red embroidery floss or yarn, make 2 short stitches for the mouth. Place 2 tiny stitches over the center of the mouth stitches to secure them.

5. Wrap red yarn around the neck for a scarf.

6. Stitch on 3 black beads for buttons or embroider with black embroidery floss or yarn.

7. Weave all yarn ends inside the snowman.

Yarn

- Weft: Atlantic by Briggs & Little (100% pure wool; 4 oz./113 g, 135 yd./123 m), #02 Washed White, 1 ball

Other Materials

- 2 black beads ¼" (6 mm) in diameter or black embroidery floss, for eyes
- 1 small pink heart button ½" (1.3 cm) in diameter, for nose
- yarn or embroidery floss for mouth
- stuffing

Body and Head

Weave the Pegagurumi Basic Body and Head (see page 106) with 1 strand of white yarn. Use white warp strands for the white head and body. Stitch the pieces together.

Tail, Arms, Legs, and Ears

For the arms, legs, and tail, make 5 half hitch spirals with white yarn following instructions for the half hitch spirals on page 108. Stitch them to the body.

For the ears, make 2 half hitch spirals following the directions on page 108, but don't pull them up as firmly—you want these about 2" (5 cm) long.

Final Steps

1. For the ears: Use the warp strand ends to stitch the ears to the bunny's head. Weave the weft ends inside the head.

2. For the nose: Stitch the pink heart button to the middle of the face.

3. For the mouth: Take 2 small straight stitches, one on top of each other, then make 1 tiny stitch over the middle of them to secure them.

4. For the eyes: Stitch 2 beads to the face or embroider black eyes with contrasting black embroidery floss or glossy yarn.

5. For the tail: Fold the half hitch spiral in half and stitch it to the bunny's bottom.

6. Take all ends inside the bunny.

Frog

Yarn

- Weft: Atlantic by Briggs & Little (100% pure wool; 4 oz./113 g, 135 yd./123 m), #30 Fern Green, 1 ball

Other Materials

- 2 black beads or buttons ½" (1.3 cm) in diameter or black embroidery floss, for eyes
- yarn or embroidery floss for mouth
- stuffing

Body, Arms, Legs, and Head

Weave the Pegagurumi Basic Body, Arms and Legs, and Head (see page 106) with 1 strand of yarn. Stitch them together.

Eyelids

Make eyelids for the frog following the directions for the Koala Ears (see page 117).

Finishing

1. For the eyes: Use the warp strand ends to stitch the eyelids to the frog's head. Weave the weft ends inside the head. Stitch the buttons or beads to the eyelids.

2. For the mouth: Make 2 small straight stitches, 1 on top of the other. Then place 1 tiny stitch over the middle to secure them.

3. Add 2 long stitches on both sides of the short stitches to make a long smile.

4. Take all ends inside the frog.

Teddy Bear

Yarn

• Weft: Atlantic by Briggs & Little (100% pure wool; 4 oz./113 g, 135 yd./123 m), #36 Gold, 1 ball

Other Materials

• 2 black beads ¼" (6 mm) in diameter or black embroidery floss, for eyes
• yarn or embroidery floss for nose and mouth
• stuffing

CONSTRUCTION

Follow the instructions for the Panda (see page 119), omitting the eye patches. Embroider the Teddy Bear's nose and mouth with black yarn or embroidery floss.

Octopus

Yarn

- Weft: Atlantic by Briggs & Little (100% pure wool; 4 oz./113 g, 135 yd./123 m), #448 Hunter Orange, 1 ball

Other Materials

- 2 black beads ¼" (6 mm) in diameter or black embroidery floss, for eyes
- ½" (1.3 cm) pink heart-shaped button
- stuffing

Body and Head

Weave the Pegagurumi Basic Body and Head (see page 106) with 1 strand of yarn. Stitch them together.

Legs

Make 8 half hitch spirals that are each 2" (5 cm) long. The tail of yarn will need to be about 4" (10 cm) long to allow for the extra length. When finishing the spiral, pull the spirals up very gently to make the finished coil of half hitch knots longer.

Final Steps

1. For the legs: Use the warp strand ends to stitch the legs to the lower edge of the octopus's body. Weave the yarn ends inside the body.

2. For the mouth: Stitch a pink heart-shaped button on the middle of the face.

3. For the eyes: Stitch 2 beads to the face or embroider black eyes with contrasting black embroidery floss or glossy yarn.

4. Take all ends inside the octopus.

Owl

Yarn

- Weft: Atlantic by Briggs & Little (100% pure wool; 4 oz./113 g, 135 yd./123 m), #25 Fawn and #36 Gold, 1 ball each.

Other Materials

- 2 black beads ¼" (6 mm) in diameter or black embroidery floss, for eyes
- stuffing

Body and Head

Weave the Pegagurumi Basic Body and Head (see page 106) with 1 strand of white yarn. Use white warp strands for the white head and body. Stitch them together.

Forehead and Wings

Weave 3 leaf shapes with brown yarn, following the instructions on page 78.

Eyes

Make 2 half hitch circles with gold yarn using 1 peg. See the instructions on page 9.

Finishing

1. For the forehead: Pin the leaf shape to the owl's head.

2. For the eyes: Stitch the gold circles to the face so they are partially covered by the forehead, then stitch the forehead in place.

3. Stitch 2 black ¼" (6 mm)-diameter beads to the eyes or embroider black eyes with contrasting black embroidery floss or glossy yarn.

4. For the beak: Push the weft strands on the point of the face piece up to both sides of the point, exposing the warp strands.

5. With gold yarn, embroider over the point of the leaf shape for the mouth. Weave in the ends.

6. For the wings: Fold the leaf shapes slightly and stitch them to the body.

7. Weave all yarn ends inside the owl.

CHAPTER 7

Working with Color

Working with more than one color to create patterns and images is exciting and inspiring. The basic techniques can be a little challenging, but mastering a few ways of joining color areas and weaving shapes will enable you to design and weave complex pieces that are incredibly rewarding and satisfying.

How to Work with Templates and Patterns

When weaving tapestry and color work on peg looms, working with a template, a pattern, or a cartoon can be helpful. You're probably familiar with the terms "template" (a full-size rendering of a finished piece or a smaller guide to one particular shape/element) and "pattern" (a diagram of steps). The term "cartoon" within the context of peg looms may be unfamiliar. A cartoon is the name given to the line drawing or pattern for a tapestry. Templates and cartoons are both forms of patterns.

When you weave a larger piece, like the screen on page 167, using a template ensures that the finished weaving will be exactly the right length and the design elements in the finished piece will be correctly shaped and proportioned. This accuracy is especially beneficial when several pieces need to be the same length.

Scaling a Freehand Template from a Sketch or Small Drawing

These instructions will show you how to create a grid-line that will allow you to enlarge or decrease a sketch or other artwork to fit a specific size for a weaving project. The instructions are based on scaling up the sketch for the Trees in Four Seasons Screen on page 167. But these instructions work whenever you are scaling a small sketch up to a larger size.

1. Calculate the size of the finished object you wish to weave, and then cut a piece of brown paper to size to make the template. Fold it in half horizontally and then vertically. With a pencil, lightly sketch lines along the folds. Fold the edges to the center, first horizontally and then vertically, and sketch these folds in very lightly. These lines will create a grid for sketching the pattern. If you want to add more lines, feel free to do so.

2. Print, scan, or trace the pattern. Trim away the excess paper. Follow the same procedure in step 1 to make a grid on the pattern.

3. Decide how much of the piece will be occupied by dominant elements. In this example, I focused on the hills, the canopy of trees, and the trunks. Make marks on the template to establish where each element will be and then sketch them in with pencil. Follow the grid, drawing one square at a time, for clarity.

4. Hold the template up frequently to see how it looks when it's vertical, as it will look very different than when it's lying horizontally on a table.

5. When you are satisfied with your template, draw over the pattern lines with a permanent marker. Erase all of the pencil lines.

Scaling a Template Using Graph Paper

Use these instructions to enlarge or decrease a template with graph paper. The Cozy Roving Shawl on page 161 is used as an example.

1. Purchase paper that has 1" (2.5 cm) squares already printed on it, or draw 1" (2.5 cm) squares on large sheets of paper that are slightly larger than the finished size of the template for your project.

2. Number the squares matching the numbers on the templates for the project.

3. Match each line in the small scale illustration by drawing it on the same square on your scaled-up graph paper.

How to Change the Size of a Template

The patterns in this book are drawn to a scale of ¼" (6 mm) = 1" (2.5 cm). If you feel that the project is too small for you and you want to weave it larger, then draw your squares 1¼" (3.2 cm) or 1½" (3.75 cm). This scale will make the finished project 25 or 50 percent larger than the original project in the photos. If it is too large, scale down the project simply by drawing your squares ¾" (1.9 cm) or ½" (1.3 cm) instead of 1" (2.5 cm) square. Be sure to number the squares exactly the same way they are in the diagram.

Weaving Shaped Pieces with a Template

If you are weaving a piece that has a shaped edge, always start working from the straight edge of the template.

1. Weave a foundation of approximately 1" (2.5 cm) while holding the template against the pegs at the end of each row to make sure that you are following the template.

2. After you have woven 1" (2.5 cm), push the edge of the template up against the back of the pegs, pushing the foundation rows down to the base of the pegs. Hold the template in place with a clothespin or small spring clamp at each outside edge.

3. Move the clothespins up the pegs as the weaving moves upward.

4. When the pegs are full and the warp needs to be advanced, use a pencil to make a mark at each edge at the top of the weaving. Then take the clothespins off and lift the template away from the pegs.

5. Fold the template at the marks. Make sure the fold line is perpendicular to the edges so the weaving stays in line with the template and doesn't go off at an angle.

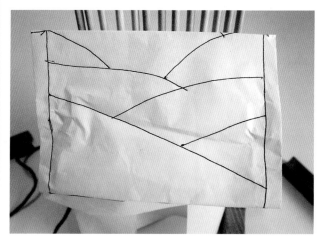

6. Advance the warp strands and place the pegs back into the holes.

7. Push the template up against the back of the pegs and use the clothespins to hold the completed part of the template to the weaving that is against the back of the pegs. The fold of the template needs to be right against the base of the pegs.

8. When you have woven ½"–1" (1.3–2.5 cm), clip the clothespins to the pegs at the weaving.

9. When the top of the template is an angle, pull the peg(s) that will no longer be woven out of its hole(s). Pull up several inches of warp yarn, and then drop them to the front of the loom so they won't get tangled into the weaving when you advance the weaving.

10. When weaving several pieces from the same template, the folds in the template are convenient, as you won't have to draw lines and make new fold lines.

Eccentric Wefts

Eccentric wefts or color changes are the easiest to make in tapestry weaving, as there are no joins or interlocks. Unlike vertical color changes, these color blocks are created by weaving the weft strands over one or a few more warp strands at a time to create the diagonal lines in the shapes. In this color work technique the blocks of color don't reach from side to side of the loom. Also, they can begin and end in the middle of the loom and are built up in short rows to form blocks of color. The rows can arch over other shapes. The only hard and fast rule is that one shape has to be built over the previous ones so they are supported by the weaving you've already done.

How to Make Vertical Color Changes

Vertical changes are made when there is a straight vertical line between two different colors. Vertical joins—where these colors abut—are one of the keys to weaving tapestries. Making the vertical join requires that you check to see if the weft will be able to weave back in its next pass (go around the peg it needs to travel around) without pulling up the other color of weft and making a vertical stitch between the pegs. If it captures the other color and they can both travel past their next pegs and both move back in their next pass without a vertical stitch being formed, then the join is correct.

If the result is a vertical stitch, the join is not correct.

To correct it, take the color over the other color instead of under it.

An alternative to making vertical joins is to weave each section separately, leaving a gap between the sections. Then you can stitch the sections together when the project is complete.

How to Weave Geometric Patterns

Weaving with more than one color allows you to create beautiful patterns that look far more complex than they really are. You can weave geometric patterns on full-size peg looms (for wider pieces) or on just a few weaving sticks (for narrow pieces). Some of the patterns work better with an odd number of weaving sticks or pegs.

Warping the Loom or Sticks

Warp the desired number of weaving sticks or pegs with the required warp strands. The warp yarn can be a contrasting color if desired for a decorative element, or it can match one of the colors of weft. The warp ends can be woven in, twisted and knotted for a fringe, or made into yarn babies.

Color Change Floats

Usually when weaving geometric patterns, only one color is worked in small blocks at a time. When another color is needed for the next shape, the previous color is dropped, then will pass for a short distance behind the other. If the distance is too long to float the color, or if multiple colors are being used, then you'll want to snip the yarn, tie a knot, and weave in the ends. Always take the color that needs to be floated to the back so all floats will be on the same side.

Self-striping or self-patterning yarns will yield stripes or color blocks, depending on the length of the color segments in the yarn and how many weaving sticks or pegs you are using.

When weaving wider widths, it is often a good idea to have many separate strands of weft yarn for each color block. The weft can be wrapped around a clothespin or embroidery bobbin or left as a loose strand. The points where the different colors meet can be interlocked (as in the Butterfly Table Mat on page 156) or they can float from row to row.

Horizontal Stripes

Horizontal stripes offer lots of room to experiment. You can choose to use only two colors or many, then weave several rows of one color and several rows of another color or alternate the numbers of rows and colors at random. You can also decide to weave a uniform number of rows to create equal width stripes or varied widths to render stripes that are different widths.

Vertical Stripes

1. Each of the 2 colors of weft must follow its own path to create vertical stripes. Make a half hitch knot with color 1 and place it on the right-hand edge weaving stick (or just continue with a color that is already on the weaving sticks).

2. Make a half hitch knot with color 2 and place it on the left-hand side edge weaving stick.

3. With color 1 on the right-hand edge weaving stick, weave across to the left-hand side. Drop color 1.

4. Pick up color 2 at the left-hand edge weaving stick and weave across to the right-hand side. Drop color 2.

5. Weave color 1 back to the right-hand side. Weave color 2 back to the left-hand side.

6. Color 2 always passes under color 1 so that the 2 colors will lock around each other at the edge to keep the continuity of the pattern.

7. Repeat steps 3–5 for the desired depth of the vertical stripes.

8. When the vertical stripes are long enough, make a half hitch knot and cut the yarn, leaving a 2"–3" (5–7.5 cm) tail.

Checkerboard

1. Weave approximately ½" (1.3 cm) (or your choice of size for the checkerboard pattern) of vertical stripes.

2. To shift the colors to make the second set of checks, weave across the weaving sticks with either color a second time so it will reverse the orientation of the over/under sequence of the colors.

3. Weave the same number of rows as in the first block of checks.

4. Repeat steps 1–3.

5. You can also make longer checked patterns, as well as the classic checkerboard.

Diagonal Stripes

Diagonal stripes can slant in either direction. The sampler in the photos was woven on 7 weaving sticks, but diagonal stripes can be woven on any number of weaving sticks or pegs.

Make a half hitch knot around the right-hand edge weaving stick or tie the yarn to a previous color with a square knot.

1. Begin by weaving a tiny triangle at the right-hand side of the weaving sticks:

Weave 3 rows on 3 weaving sticks.

Weave 3 rows on 2 weaving sticks.

Wrap the right-hand edge weaving stick three times.

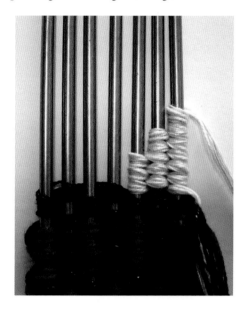

2. Take the next color behind the starting triangle.

Weave 3 rows on the next 3 weaving sticks.

Move up and over 1 weaving stick and weave 3 rows on 3 weaving sticks.

Continue to move to the right and up, ending by weaving 3 rows on 2 weaving sticks.

Wrap the right-hand side edge weaving stick three times.

3. Weave the third and all subsequent stripes.

Take the next color behind the previous stripe to the left-hand side weaving stick. Wrap it three times.

Weave 3 rows on 2 weaving sticks.

Weave 3 rows on 3 weaving sticks.

Move up and over 1 weaving stick and weave 3 rows on 3 weaving sticks.

Continue to move to the right and up, ending by weaving 3 rows on 2 weaving sticks.

Wrap the right-hand side edge weaving stick three times.

4. Repeat steps 1–3 for the desired length.

The floats on the wrong side of the weaving can be snipped after the weaving is complete, then woven in or left if the wrong side of the weaving is not going to be seen.

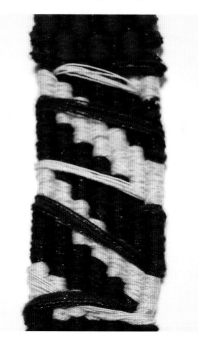

Triangles

1. The triangles in this sample are built on a half triangle base. Begin by weaving a half triangle for the base of the pattern:

With color 1 at the left-hand side of the weaving sticks, weave 3 rows on all 7 weaving sticks.

Weave 3 rows on 6 weaving sticks.

Weave 3 rows on 5 weaving sticks.

Weave 3 rows on 4 weaving sticks.

Weave 3 rows on 3 weaving sticks.

Weave 3 rows on 2 weaving sticks.

Wrap the left-hand edge weaving stick three times.

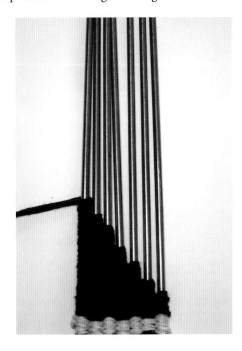

2. Begin weaving the full triangles:

With color 2 at the right-hand side, wrap the right-hand edge weaving stick three times.

Weave 3 rows on 2 weaving sticks.

Weave 3 rows on 3 weaving sticks.

Weave 3 rows on 4 weaving sticks.

Weave 3 rows on 5 weaving sticks.

Weave 3 rows on 6 weaving sticks.

Weave 3 rows on all 7 weaving sticks.

Weave 3 rows on 6 weaving sticks.

Weave 3 rows on 5 weaving sticks.

Weave 3 rows on 4 weaving sticks.

Weave 3 rows on 3 weaving sticks.

Weave 3 rows on 2 weaving sticks.

Wrap the right-hand edge weaving stick three times. This completes the first triangle.

3. With color 1 at the left-hand edge, weave the next triangle, moving the shaping out and back from the left-hand edge.

4. Continue weaving triangles in this manner to the desired length.

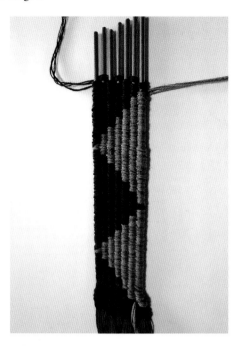

Diamonds

The diamond pattern is woven on an odd number of weaving sticks. In the photos, 7 weaving sticks are used.

1. Begin with color 1 at the right-hand side and weave across all the weaving sticks with color 1 for 5 rows.

2. Make the right-hand lower triangle: Weave 3 rows (or more if you prefer) on 3 weaving sticks. The center weaving stick has to stay empty for now.

  Weave 3 rows on 2 weaving sticks at the right-hand edge. Wrap the right-hand edge weaving stick three times.

3. Weave loosely across all the weaving sticks, angling down the hypotenuse of the triangle and across the remaining 4 weaving sticks to the left-hand edge.

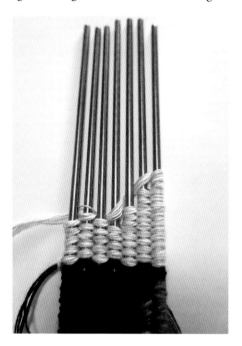

4. Make the left-hand lower triangle: Weave 3 rows on 3 weaving sticks.

  Weave 3 rows on 2 weaving sticks at the left-hand side. Wrap the left edge weaving stick three times.

5. Drop color 1.

6. Pick up color 2 and bring it to the front of the weaving sticks to the left of the center weaving stick.

7. Wrap the center weaving stick three times.

8. Weave 3 rows on 3 weaving sticks, ending at the right-hand side.

9. Take the yarn to the front of the weaving stick adjacent to the last weaving stick and around to the back.

10. Weave 3 rows on 5 weaving sticks, ending at the right-hand side.

11. Weave 3–7 rows (depending on how tall you want the diamond to be) on all 7 weaving sticks for the center of the diamond.

12. Work the top half of the diamond: Weave 3 rows, skipping 1 weaving stick at each side edge of the diamond until you reach the center weaving stick.

Wrap it three times.

13. Drop color 2.

14. Pick up color 1 and bring it up between the first and second weaving sticks on the left-hand side.

Wrap the edge weaving stick three times.

Weave 3 rows on 2 weaving sticks.

Weave 3 rows on 3 weaving sticks.

15. Weave loosely all the way across the weaving sticks to the right-hand side. Ease the yarn down the slope of the diamond.

Wrap the edge weaving stick three times.

Weave 3 rows on 2 weaving sticks.

Weave 3 rows on 3 weaving sticks.

16. Weave to the edge and repeat the pattern for the next diamond.

Weaving Narrow Bands

Throughout history, narrow looms have been used to weave fabric of any desired width.

How? Simply by stitching together narrow bands to create cloth of great beauty and complexity. Weaving narrow bands on a few weaving sticks allows you to experiment with color and pattern and practice your skills at weaving geometric motifs before moving on to wider pieces.

Woven narrow bands that are a single color are often placed between complex patterned bands to set off the slower-to-weave patterned bands and highlight them. Single color bands are quicker to weave than multicolor bands. They make an excellent take-along project for on-the-go weaving because you have only one color of weft to take with you.

Narrow bands can be used to make anything you can weave on a wider loom: vests, coats, bags, pillows, chair seats, throws, shawls, dolls, jewelry, baskets . . . The only limit is your imagination, and the result is a wonderful, vibrant, and unique woven fabric.

Tip Weave several bands before you begin stitching them together so you can experiment with the placement of the bands.

Celebration Chair Seat

The fabric in the photo was inspired by a chair purchased from a thrift shop. The whimsical paint was charming, but faded. Once I touched up the colors, the chair came to life. Unfortunately, the stains on the upholstery of the seat didn't respond to attempts at cleaning, so a cover was necessary.

Equipment

- 4, 5, 6, or 7 weaving sticks of any size, or pegs from a peg loom
- small latch hook
- warp threader
- scissors
- tape measure
- Steel weaving sticks from Daegrad Tools were used for the project in the photo. Because they are very slender (⅛" [3 mm] in diameter), a very fine sett can be achieved when using thin yarns like ⅜ weaving cotton, crochet cotton, lace, or sock weight yarns.

Yarn

- Warp: ⅜ weaving cotton or crochet cotton of any color or colors
- Weft: ⅜ weaving cotton or crochet cotton, sock yarn or any yarn of your choice, or embroidery floss
- Warp the sticks with 4 strands held together. Hold multiple strands of thin threads and yarns together to make a thicker yarn. This allows you to blend colors and speeds up weaving. Weaving with a single strand of weaving cotton or crochet cotton is very slow, but gives a pleasing fabric. If you need the project to move along quickly, more strands held together can be a good choice.

Specs

- WPI: 9 or 10 wraps per 1" (2.5 cm) for single or combined yarns
- Finished Measurement: Approximately 19" x 15" (48 x 38 cm)
- Weaving a narrow band is an excellent way to produce a swatch to check to see exactly how many pegs will give you the correct dimensions with the warp and weft yarns that you have chosen, as well as to check tension, sett, bloom, or draw in.

WEAVING

See How to Weave with Weaving Sticks on page 14 and How to Weave Color Change Patterns on page 131.

FINISHING

Work yarn babies on the warp strands, see page 23.
  Stitch the narrow bands together.

Bag for a Yoga Mat or Peg Loom

Here's another fun opportunity to hone your geometric pattern weaving skills. This lovely bag is handy for carrying and stashing your yoga mat, water bottle, towel, and other items that need to be organized for yoga or Pilates. It also works well to store the base of your peg loom, assorted pegs, accessories, and notebooks all together in between weaving projects.

Equipment

- Dewberry Ridge 6" (15 cm)-wide peg loom
- 8 medium-size pegs, ¼" (6 mm) in diameter
- 10" (25 cm) Dewberry Ridge weaving sticks, ¼" (6 mm) in diameter (7 weaving sticks are used to weave the bands for the sides, so 2 sets of 6 pegs are required—or use 7 pegs on your peg loom)
- tape measure
- scissors
- warp threader
- blunt tapestry needle
- latch hook

Yarn

- Warp: #4 medium weight acrylic yarn, 2 balls, 1.7 oz./50 g each
- Weft: Unique by Lion Brand, #5 bulky weight (100% acrylic; 3.5 oz./100 g, 109 yd./100 m), #201 Garden, 2 balls; Vanna's Choice by Lion Brand, #4 medium weight (100% acrylic; 3.5 oz./100 g, 170 yd./156 m), Black, 2 balls

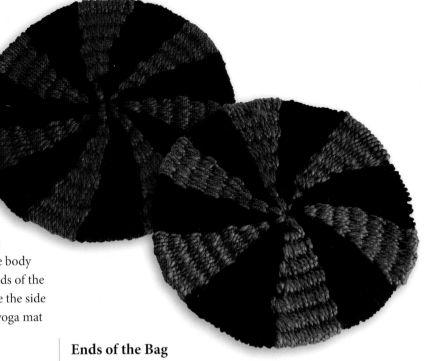

Specs

- WPI: 9 wraps per 1" (2.5 cm)
- Finished Measurements: Approximately 7" (17.5 cm) in diameter by 27" (67.5 cm) long with a 36" (90 cm) long shoulder strap
- The body of the bag is woven on 7 weaving sticks, or pegs from a peg loom, in narrow bands. See page 155 for instructions on how to weave color change patterns. If you prefer, you can weave the bands without patterning them. Or, you can weave the body of the bag as one piece on a larger loom. The ends of the bag are circles (see page 35). You can also weave the side section shorter if your loom is shorter or your yoga mat is narrower.

Body of the Bag

SETUP

Use 2 strands of warp for each weaving stick. The working length of the warp strands is 39" (97.5 cm). The cut length is 78" (195 cm).

WEAVING

With 7 weaving sticks or pegs and both weft yarns, weave the geometric pattern(s) of your choice following the instructions on page 131. Weave 7 bands that are approximately 3" (7.5 cm) wide by 27" (67.5 cm) long.

Ends of the Bag

SETUP

Use 2 strands of warp for each weaving stick.

The working length for the left-hand peg (outside edge) is 39" (97.5 cm). The cut length is 78" (195 cm). The remaining 7 pegs can have shorter working lengths that are staggered down to 12" (30 cm) for the right-hand (center of the circle) peg.

WEAVING

Using 8 pegs on the peg loom and both colors of weft yarn, weave 2 circles, following the instructions for weaving pinwheel circles on page 39.

Strap

SETUP

Use 3 strands of warp for each weaving stick. The working length of the warp strands is 44" (110 cm). The cut length is 88" (220 cm).

WEAVING

With 4 weaving sticks or pegs and both weft yarns, weave 1 band that is approximately 1¾" (4.5 cm) wide by 36" (90 cm) long with fringes that are about 4" (10 cm) long at each end. (See page 133 for how to weave triangles.) Weave the strap very densely, packing in lots of weft.

Following the instructions on page 23, make a yarn baby at both ends of the strap.

Buttons (Make 3)

With 3 strands of yarn for the warp and with 2 strands of yarn held together for the weft, make 3 buttons that are about 2" (5 cm) in diameter. (See page 52 for instructions to make buttons.)

Button Loop Cords (Make 3)

WEAVING

1. Use 2 strands of warp. The working length of the warp strands for the button loop cords is 15" (37.5 cm). The cut length is 30" (75 cm).

2. Following instructions on page 24 for single peg/ weaving stick half hitch cords, make a half hitch cord 5" (12.5 cm) long with warp ends at both ends of the cord that are 5" (12.5 cm). Snip the warp ends from the peg.

3. Holding the weft ends together with the warp ends at each end of the cord, tie a knot to secure the ends and form the button loop.

Finishing

1. Stitch the 7 bands together to make a rectangle that is 21" (52.5 cm) wide by 27" (67.5 cm) long to form the body of the bag.

2. Pin the body of the bag to the end circles. Stitch ends to body of bag, leaving the long edges open.

3. Stitch the handles to the seam at the ends of the opening.

4. Stitch the buttons to the bag, as shown in the photos. (See page 33.)

5. Matching the button placement, stitch the button loops on the open edge of the bag.

Take half the warp ends through the front of the weaving to the wrong side and half of them through the wrong side to the right side of the fabric.

Take the ends on the right side of the bag ½" (1.3 cm) down and then back through to the wrong side of the bag.

Tie a very firm knot with the yarn ends.

Weave the yarn ends into the fabric of the bag.

Rolling Hills Tapestry

The his small tapestry is a perfect project to learn the process of weaving a simple image with a peg loom. I designed it so the rolling hills are all horizontal in orientation, with no vertical lines, so one hill acts as the foundation for the ones above it.

A good place to begin the Rolling Hills Tapestry is by printing out several copies of the cartoon (pattern) and coloring it with felts, crayons, or watercolor paints to give you a sense of which colors will give you the effect you are looking for. For instance, there can be a lake or a stream. It can be a night sky or sunrise or sunset. The circle can be the sun or moon, or take it out completely and the tapestry becomes a moment at midday. The shapes at the top of the cartoon can be trees or hills or clouds. The decisions are totally up to you.

Working with this small cartoon will make working with a larger template feel much more comfortable. Feel free to scale up this small cartoon and add more details.

Equipment

- 6" (15 cm)-wide peg loom or any size peg loom of your choice
- 13 fine-size pegs, ³⁄₁₆" (4 mm) in diameter
- tape measure
- scissors
- warp threader
- blunt tapestry needle
- long glass-top pins or T-pins
- large sewing needle and black sewing thread
- pencil or pen
- felt-tip pens or crayons or watercolor paints
- tracing paper or waxed paper or a printer
- latch hook
- 2 clothespins
- plastic or metal cabone rings to be stitched to the back of the finished piece for hanging
- steam iron
- felting needle and fleece (optional)

Yarn

- Warp: #4 medium weight acrylic yarn, 2 balls, 1.7 oz./50 g each
- Weft: Atlantic by Briggs & Little (100% pure wool; 4 oz./113 g, 135 yd./123 m), #64 Khaki, #62 Green Heather, #18 Grey Heather, #42 Blue Heather, #36 Gold, #61 Dark Green, #65 Paddy Green, and #76 Red Heather, 1 ball each

Specs

- WPI: 8 wraps per 1" (2.5 cm)
- Finished Measurements: 8" (20 cm) tall by 5" (12.5 cm) wide
- If you want to weave the Rolling Hills Tapestry on a larger loom, using larger pegs, simply scale the template up in size to match your loom. See How to Work with Templates and Patterns on page 129.

Notes

Use a felting needle to add details with roving or fleece after the weaving is complete and all the warp ends are woven in.

SETUP

1. Warp: Use 1 strand of warp for each peg. The working length of the warp strands is 18" (40 cm). The cut length is 36" (80 cm).

2. Scan and print or trace a copy of the Rolling Hills Tapestry Template onto tracing paper or waxed paper. Trim it so the border at the lower edge of the cartoon is at least 1" (2.5 cm). Fold the side edges back from the cartoon, leaving a narrow border around the sides.

WEAVING

1. Following the instructions on page 129 for working with a template, begin by weaving the first ½" (1.3 cm) with your choice of color.

2. Place a clothespin at each side to hold the template in place.

3. Note that the first color starts to move to the left-hand side. This means that you will be leaving pegs at the right-hand side of the loom empty. Follow the line on the template to weave the first shape.

4. Finish with a half hitch knot at the right-hand side of the loom. Cut the first color off.

5. Work the weft ends to the back of the weaving.

6. The second shape fits over the first shape and will provide a foundation for the third shape.

7. The third shape is built on the second and first shapes.

8. The fourth shape is built on the first and third shapes.

9. The fifth shape is mostly over the third shape, but is also a little bit over the fourth. It cannot be woven until the fourth shape is complete, because it would block access to the pegs in the right-hand side of the fourth shape.

10. Weave the sixth shape.

11. Weaving section 7: Weave up to the 2 arrows on the template, which are a suggestion of a good place to stop, and then take the clothespins off the loom.

Rolling Hills Tapestry Template

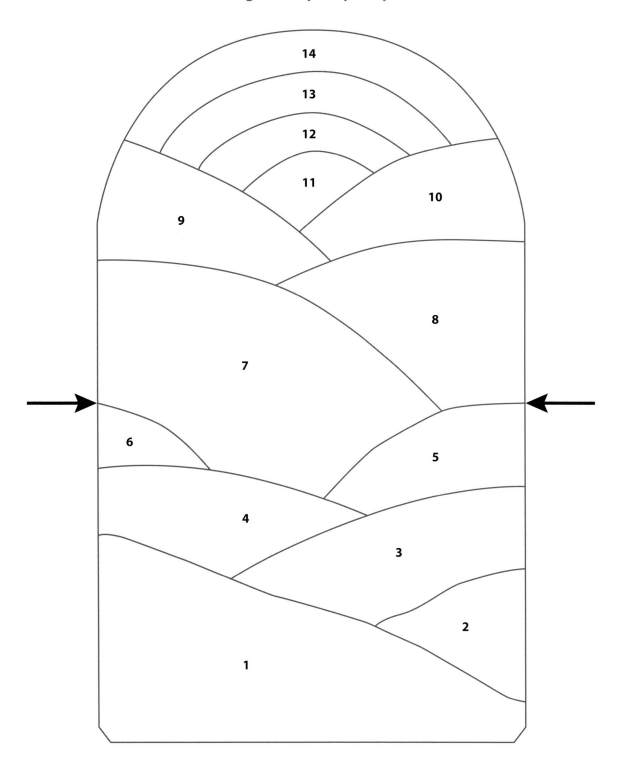

12. Fold the template at the arrows.

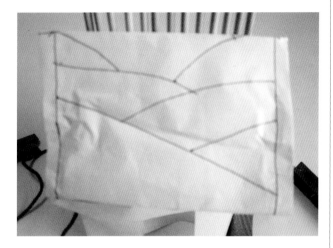

13. Use the clothespins to hold the finished part of the template (the folded-down part) to the weaving so the fold is at the base of the loom.

14. Finish weaving section number 7.

15. Move the clothespins onto the pegs and weave section 8.

16. The upper edge shaping begins when weaving sections 9 and 10.

17. Remove 1 peg at each side as the curve progresses at the top of the weaving.

18. After weaving the sun, the remaining colors are woven in an arch shape over the sun.

FINISHING

1. Remove the weaving from the loom and lay it on the template. Adjust the weaving along the warp strands to make sure the weaving is the same size and shape as the template.

2. Cut the pegs off the warp strands and work the double Damascus edge (see page 17) along the upper and lower edges.

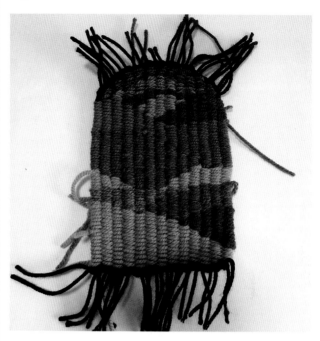

3. Weave in the warp and weft ends.

4. *Optional:* Use a felting needle to add wisps of clouds or other features. The Rolling Hills Tapestry on the right-hand side of the photo on page 145 was woven in hand-spun yarn and also had black lines embroidered between sections.

5. Stitch a ring to the back for hanging.

Upholstered Chair

Did the cat claw the corners of your chair? Or is the upholstery just worn out and tired? Why not bring the chair back to life with fabric woven on your peg loom? This exuberant fabric was woven with a combination of eccentric weft rolling hill shapes and geometric patterning. You could weave a more serene fabric in stripes or vertical lines or checks or use the rambunctious eccentric weft shapes with a quieter color palette.

Equipment

- Dewberry Ridge 24" (60 cm)-wide peg loom
- 30 medium-size pegs, ⅜" (9 mm) in diameter
- tape measure and 2 paper clamps
- scissors
- warp threader
- blunt tapestry needle
- long glass-top pins or T-pins
- large sewing needle and heavy-duty thread
- sewing machine
- latch hook
- curved upholstery needle

Yarn

- Warp: #4 medium weight acrylic yarn, 3 balls, 1.7 oz./50 g each
- Weft: Super by Briggs & Little (100% pure wool; 4 oz./113 g, 85 yd./78 m), #64 Khaki, #56 Mauve, #82 Pink, #72 Light Maroon, #13 Light Grey, #45 Peacock, #61 Dark Green, #30 Fern Green, and #44 Teal, 2 balls each

Specs

- WPI: 7 wraps per 1" (2.5 cm)
- Finished Measurements:
  - Chair seat: Approximately 22" (56 cm) by 23" (58.5 cm)
  - Sides of seat: 4" (10 cm) tall
  - Back of chair: Tape measure wrapped around the back measures 36½" (92 cm)
  - Sides of back: 2½" (6 cm) deep, 10" (25 cm) tall above the arms, and 4" (10 cm) tall below the arms
- The seat of the project chair was woven from the lower back edge to the lower front edge. The side sections were woven separately. The back section was woven in one piece that wraps entirely around the front and back of the upper part of the chair.

SETUP

Measure your chair and make notes of which pieces can be woven as a continuous piece and which ones will need to be warped and woven separately. Weave a gauge swatch and determine the setup for each of the pieces you will need to weave.

WEAVING

Following the instructions for your desired pattern and the setup needed to get the desired size, warp and weave each of the pieces of fabric for the chair.

ASSEMBLY

1. For the upper back section: Place the weaving on the chair, match up the ends of each channel, and tie the first part of surgeon's knots (see page 10) across the chair. Tighten the knots as necessary. Then tie the second half of the knots on all sets of warp strands.

2. Work the double Damascus edge (see page 17) on all other pieces.

3. For each of the remaining pieces of fabric: Use the latch hook to pull the warp ends into the channels of the weaving.

Use paper clamps to hold the tape measure at the desired width of the fabric. Be very careful to not distort the width of the fabric.

Stitch across the fabric with the sewing machine set on the longest straight stitch.

FINISHING

1. Do not remove the previous upholstery fabric from the chair, if possible.

2. Pin and then stitch the panels to the chair, using a curved upholstery needle.

3. Stitch the side panels to the center panels.

4. Stitch the panels to the original fabric at the lower edges.

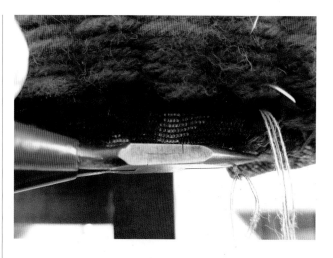

5. Measure and then make half hitch cords to cover the seams and lower edges (see page 24).

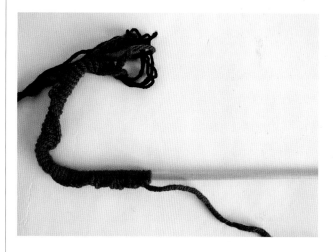

6. Stitch the cords to the chair with the curved upholstery needle.

Butterfly Table Mat

Weaving the Butterfly Table Mat is an excellent way to hone your skills for making vertical joins (see page 131) and to practice working with templates. If you aren't a fan of table mats, then change the size and shape of the woven piece and weave a bag or a pillow. You can make several smaller mats and then stitch them together for a table runner or a shawl or go even bigger and make a blanket. Don't assume that a pattern can only be one thing: Just add imagination and the sky's the limit.

The Essence of the Vertical Join

Vertical joins are intuitive. You do a quick flip of the yarns, asking yourself: Does this go over or under the other color? If it's going to catch the other color and both are able to go on to their next pass without forming a vertical stitch between the pegs at the color join, then it's right. One color should catch the other, snug it up against the peg in the space between the colors, and both will be in position to move smoothly on their way.

Butterfly Table Mat Template

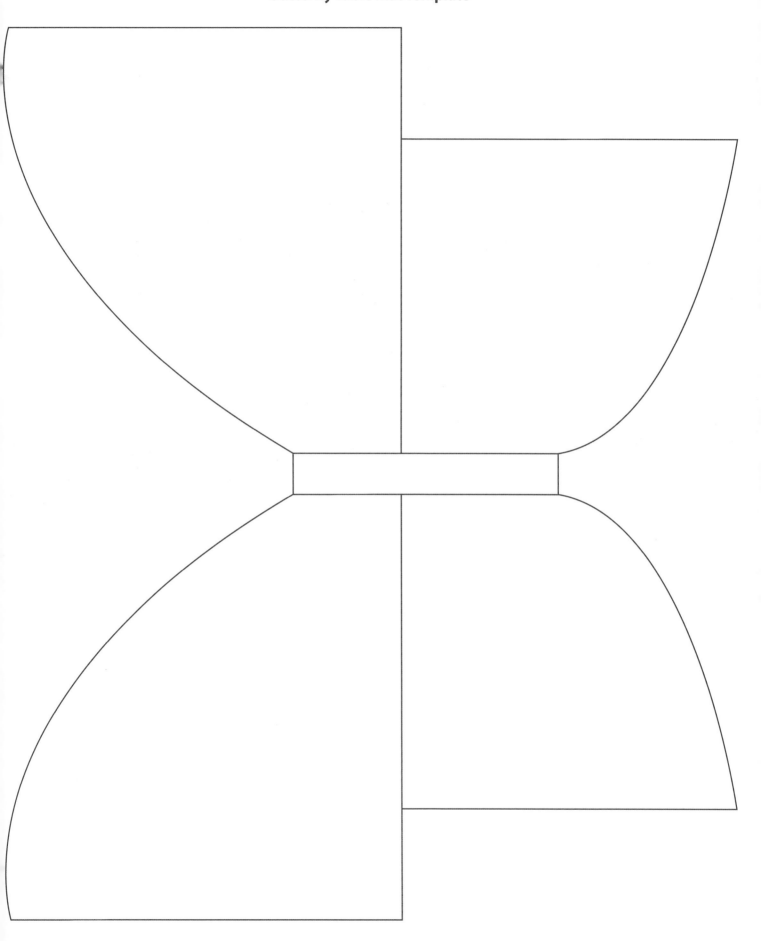

Equipment

- 15" (37.55 cm)-wide peg loom, or a loom of your choice
- 26 pegs, ¼" (6 mm) in diameter
- tape measure
- scissors
- warp threader
- blunt tapestry needle
- pencil or pen
- tracing paper or printer
- latch hook
- 2 clothespins
- steam iron

Yarn

- Color 1 (for the border and the body): Vanna's Choice by Lion Brand (92% acrylic, 8% rayon; 3 oz./85 g, 145 yd./133 m), #403 Barley, 2 balls
- Color 2 (for the butterfly): Tweed Stripes by Lion Brand (100% acrylic; 3 oz./85 g, 144 yd./132 m), #205 Caribbean, 2 balls
- Color 3 (for the contrast band): Tweed Stripes by Lion Brand (100% acrylic; 3 oz./85 g, 144 yd./132 m), #201 Orchid
- Color 4 (for the background): Tweed Stripes by Lion Brand (100% acrylic; 3 oz./85 g, 144 yd./132 m), #204 Caramel, 4 balls

Specs

- WPI: Vanna's Choice, 10 wraps per 1" (2.5 cm); Tweed Stripes, 8 wraps per 1" (2.5 cm)
- Finished Measurements: Approximately 13" (33 cm) wide by 18" (45 cm) long

Notes

- Weft: Hold 2 strands of yarn together for all weaving.
- See page 129 for a refresher on how to work with templates.
- Try making this project on a larger or smaller loom, using larger or finer pegs.

SETUP

1. Copy the butterfly pattern onto tracing paper or waxed paper. Cut a piece of paper 13" (33 cm) wide by 18" (46 cm) long. Draw a line vertically at the center of the paper and another line horizontally at the center. Glue or tape the butterfly to the center lines. (Note that the butterfly is rotated 90 degrees and worked from one wing to the other on the loom.)

2. Warp: The working length of the warp strands for each peg is 30" (75 cm). The cut length is 60" (150 cm).

WEAVING

1. Begin weaving at the left-hand side of the loom, using 2 strands of weft yarn held together. Pull the center strand of the ball out and hold it together with the outside strand to have 2 strands coming from each ball of weft yarn.

Weave 1" (2.5 cm), 6 rows of color 1 (border); cut the yarn and tie on color 4.

Weave 1" (2.5 cm), 6 rows of color 4 (background); cut the yarn and tie on color 3.

Weave ½" (1.3 cm), 3 rows of color 3 (background); cut the yarn and tie on color 4.

Weave 1" (2.5 cm), 6 rows of color 4 (background); cut the yarn and tie on color 3.

2. Use 2 clothespins to attach the template to the loom.

3. Weave the vertical color joins to make the butterfly. *Note:* There will be a vertical color join at the center of the mat, where the background color at the left side of the mat meets the butterfly color. There is a second vertical join at the point where the butterfly color meets up with the background at the right-hand side.

4. Weaving from the right to the left: Weave with the background color to the place where the butterfly begins. Bring the background to the front of the loom.

5. Drop the background color. Take one strand of the butterfly color in front of the background color and one strand behind. Tie a knot with the butterfly color.

6. Weave to the point where the right-hand edge of background color begins. Bring the butterfly color to the front and drop it.

7. Join 2 strands of background color from a second ball of yarn. Weave to the edge of the loom.

Push the yarn ends to the back. They will be woven in when the mat is finished. The color join is only made in this pass.

8. Weaving from left to right: Weave back to the point where the butterfly yarn is parked.

Take the butterfly color yarn under the background color and weave back to the background color at the left. The background color is captured by the butterfly color.

Take the left-hand background color under the butterfly and weave back to the left-hand side of the loom.

9. Repeat step 8, following the template and moving the colors where indicated by the lines.

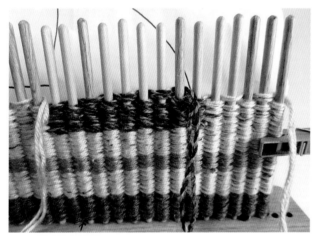

10. When the butterfly color needs to move over to the left-hand edge of the lower wing, hold the background color together with the butterfly color.

11. Drop the butterfly color at the line. Weave the background color back to the loom edge.

12. When the butterfly is complete, cut the butterfly color and finish weaving the mat:

Weave 1" (2.5 cm), 6 rows color 4 (background); cut the yarn and tie on color 3.

Weave ½" (1.3 cm), 3 rows color 3; cut the yarn and tie on color 4.

Weave 1" (2.5 cm), 6 rows color 4 (background); cut the yarn and tie on color 3.

Weave 1" (2.5 cm), 6 rows of color 1 (border); cut the yarn and tie on color 4.

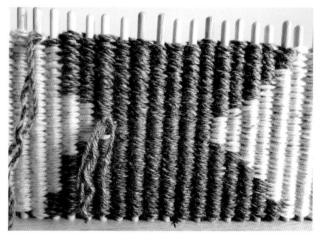

FINISHING

1. Lift the weaving off the loom and advance the warp strands.

2. Place the mat on the template and ease the mat into shape.

3. Work the double Damascus edge (see page 17) at both ends of the weaving.

4. Weave the warp ends and weft ends into the channels of the weaving.

Cozy Roving Shawl

The Cozy Roving Shawl is a chance to practice weaving vertical color changes and working with templates.

If working the color changes feels too intimidating, just work it in one color or in horizontal stripes. The options are endless. I wove the shawl in the photos with subtle shades of roving yarn, but this project would also be spectacular in vibrant jewel tones in any choice of yarn or fabric strips. The Cozy Roving Shawl looks equally spectacular draped over a sofa, hung on a wall, or wrapped around your shoulders. It could also be used as a floor mat if you cut a piece of nonslip fabric to shape and place it under the mat.

Equipment

- 24" (60 cm)-wide peg loom
- 24 pegs, ⅜" (9 mm)-diameter set on ¾" (18 mm) centers
- tape measure
- scissors
- warp threader
- blunt tapestry needle
- paper
- permanent marking pen
- large sewing needle and heavy-duty thread
- ruler and brown paper to make the templates
- latch hook

Yarn

- Warp: Atlantic by Briggs & Little (100% pure wool; 4 oz./113 g, 135 yd./123 m), #11 Dark Grey and Medium Grey, 2 balls each. Use 2 strands of yarn held together for the warp.
- Weft: Country Roving by Briggs & Little (100% pure wool; 8 oz./227 g, 85 yd./78 m), #408 Snow White, 2 balls, and #11 Dark Grey, #412 Light Grey, and #454 Sheep's Grey, 2 balls each

Specs

- WPI: 6 wraps per 1" (2.5 cm)
- Finished Measurements: Approximately 66" (165 cm) wide across the upper edge by 23" (57.5 cm) long at the center seam, or any size or shape that you prefer

Notes

- The four sections of the shawl are each woven separately, following 2 templates, and are stitched together after the weaving is complete.
- The warp strands can become the fringe or can be woven in.
- The middle of the lower edge of the shawl is rounded off to be a more flattering and comfortable shape than a long triangle. But, if you prefer, you can modify the center panel to create a triangle.
- If your peg loom is narrower than 22" (55 cm), then make more templates, weave more narrow panels, and stitch them together.
- See page 129 for information on how to work with templates.
- See page 155 for information on how to join colors.

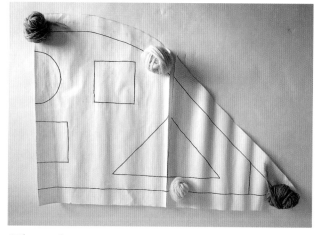

Side template

SIDE SECTIONS SETUP

Warp 24 pegs.

    Working warp length for pegs 1–6: 22" (56 cm).
        Cut length: 44" (112 cm).
    Working warp length for pegs 7–14: 26" (66 cm).
        Cut length: 52" (132 cm).
    Working warp length for pegs 15–24: 32" (82 cm).
        Cut length: 64" (164 cm).

CENTER SECTION SETUP

Warp 24 pegs with a working warp length of 40" (100 cm).
    Cut length: 80" (200 cm).

Cozy Roving Shawl Template #1

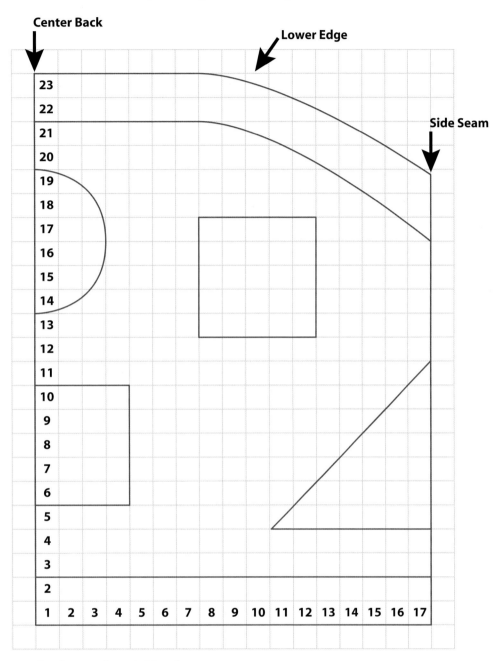

Center Back

Lower Edge

Side Seam

Begin weaving at this edge
Weave 2

1 Square = 1 inch/2.5 cm

Cozy Roving Shawl Template #2

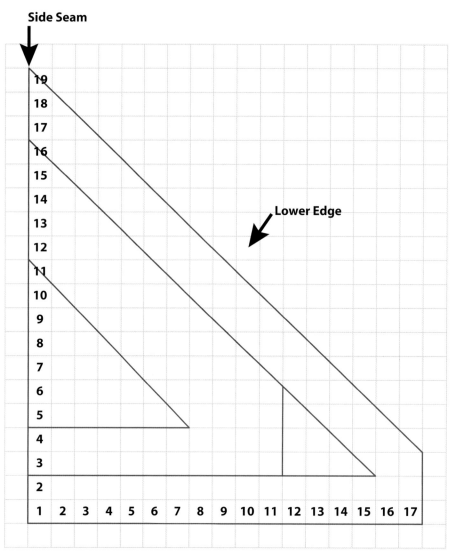

Side Seam

Lower Edge

19
18
17
16
15
14
13
12
11
10
9
8
7
6
5
4
3
2

1 2 3 4 5 6 7 8 9 10 11 12 13 14 15 16 17

Upper Edge

Begin weaving at this edge
Weave 2

1 Square = 1 inch/2.5 cm

WEAVING

1. Begin weaving at the upper edge of the templates (the straight edge).

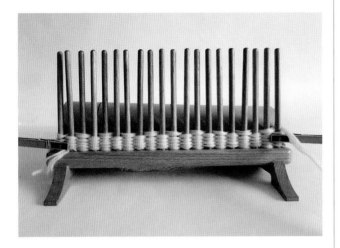

2. Weave 2 center sections and 2 side sections, following the templates.

3. Lift the weaving off the loom. Advance the warp so you have 6" (15 cm) of warp at the upper edge for finishing.

FINISHING

1. Lay the center pieces on the template to be sure that the finished dimensions are correct.

2. Trim the lower warp strands to 8" (20 cm).

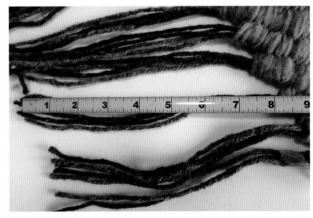

3. Stitch the center seam of the 2 middle sections.

4. Lay the side sections on the template to confirm dimensions.

5. Adjust the length of the side panels to match the center panel and pin them together.

6. Stitch the edge sections to the center of the shawl.

7. Finish the upper edge of the shawl with double Damascus knots (see page 17).

8. Weave the warp ends into the channels of the upper edge of the shawl.

9. Now work double Damascus knots along the lower edge of the shawl.

10. Lay the shawl flat and stroke the fringe out to its full length. Trim the fringe evenly.

The Trees in Four Seasons Screen is full of vertical joins. The design for this four-panel screen can be woven in any size you desire. For the screen in the photographs, I enlarged the pattern to approximately 13½" (33.75 cm) wide by 48" (120 cm) tall. The same design was woven with four different colorways to represent the four seasons.

If you're looking for alternate design ideas, try weaving the panels with colors that reflect the four elements: fire, water, earth, and air. Or, each of the panels could be woven using the same colorway. If you don't have a screen, consider mounting the panels on dowels, rods, or branches and hanging them on the wall or from a beam to act as a room divider. If you prefer, you can weave the panel just once as a wall hanging.

Equipment

- Dewberry Ridge 15" (37.5 cm)-wide peg loom or your choice of peg loom
- 28 medium-size pegs, ¼" (6 mm) in diameter
- tape measure and two paper clamps
- scissors
- warp threader
- blunt tapestry needle
- latch hook
- sturdy paper, like brown paper or freezer paper, for the template
- pencil
- eraser
- permanent fine-tip marker
- standing screen

Yarn

- Warp: #4 medium weight acrylic yarn, 3 balls, 1.8 oz./50 g each
- Weft: Atlantic by Briggs & Little (100% pure wool; 4 oz./113 g, 135 yd./123 m), #64 Khaki, #45 Peacock, #21 Brown, #22 Brown Heather, and #47 Light Blue, 2 balls each; #82 Pink, #61 Dark Green, #81 Rose, #30 Fern Green, #62 Green Heather, #14 Sheep's Grey, #32 Orange, #20 Evergreen, #25 Fawn, #73 Red, #65 Paddy Green, #37 Yellow, #31 Rust, #36 Gold, #02 Washed White, and #01 Natural White, 1 ball each

Specs

- WPI: 8 wraps per 1" (2.5 cm)
- Finished Measurements: Each woven panel of the screen is approximately 13½" (33.75 cm) wide by 48" (120 cm) tall.

Notes

- The screen panels are woven using a paper template. This type of template makes following the pattern easier and will ensure that the finished size of the panels is correct.
- See page 129 for information on how to work with templates and patterns.
- See page 155 for information on color changing techniques. The four panels were woven with colorways that corresponded to spring, summer, autumn, and winter.

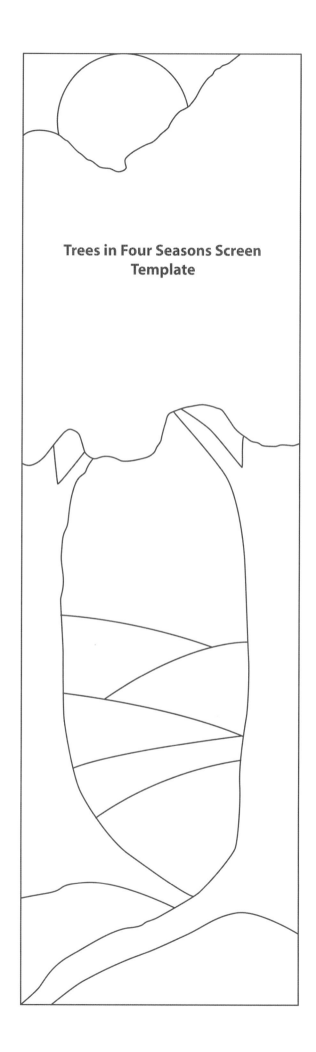

Trees in Four Seasons Screen Template

SETUP

The panels for the screen in the photos are 48" (120 cm) long, so the working length of the warp strands need to be 60" (150 cm). The cut length of each warp strand is 120" (300 cm) long. For different size panels, see page 20 to determine the length of the warp strands.

WEAVING

Weave the panels using the vertical join technique (see page 155) and following the template.

FINISHING

1. Mount the panels using the rod, dowel, or branch technique (see page 20). Knot the top of each panel to a sturdy metal rod, then insert it into the screen.

2. Knot the lower edge to a metal rod at the bottom of the screen.

Tie the warp strands with the first half of a surgeon's knot (see page 10) all the way across. Check all the warp strands for evenness, then tie the second half of the knots.

3. Advance the weaving down the warp and move the weft into place. Check it against the template to make sure that the panels are correct.

4. Weave the warp ends into the weft channels and weave in all other ends.

Gallery

I wove these tapestries and mixed weavings with peg looms, weaving sticks, and/or other looms.

Our Lady of the Waters 2012–2013
27½" (70 cm) tall by 11" (29 cm) wide
The lower half of the tapestry was woven on a
Dewberry Ridge 15" (37.5 cm)-wide peg loom
with ¼" (6 mm)-diameter pegs. The upper section was woven on Mirrix and Saori looms.

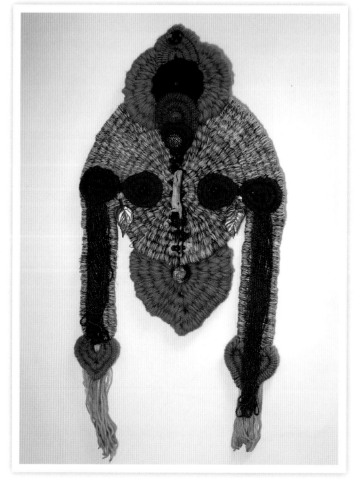

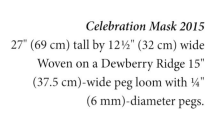

Celebration Mask 2015
27" (69 cm) tall by 12½" (32 cm) wide
Woven on a Dewberry Ridge 15"
(37.5 cm)-wide peg loom with ¼"
(6 mm)-diameter pegs.

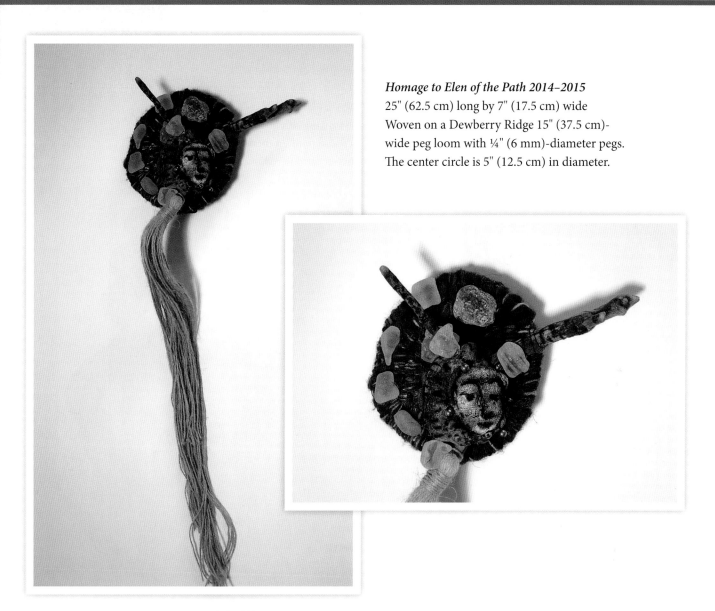

Homage to Elen of the Path 2014–2015
25" (62.5 cm) long by 7" (17.5 cm) wide
Woven on a Dewberry Ridge 15" (37.5 cm)-
wide peg loom with ¼" (6 mm)-diameter pegs.
The center circle is 5" (12.5 cm) in diameter.

The Face of Joy 2014
12" (30 cm) in diameter
Woven on a Dewberry Ridge 15"
(37.5 cm)-wide peg loom with ¼" (6 mm)-
diameter pegs.

Our Lady of the Moon and Stars 2012–2013
27" (69 cm) tall by 13" (32 cm) wide
Woven on a Dewberry Ridge 15" (37.5 cm)-wide peg loom with ¼" (6 mm)-diameter pegs. This piece includes carved and painted moose antler horn (found, not hunted) and wire hands.

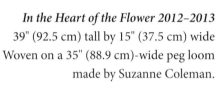

In the Heart of the Flower 2012–2013
39" (92.5 cm) tall by 15" (37.5 cm) wide
Woven on a 35" (88.9 cm)-wide peg loom made by Suzanne Coleman.

Dreaming the Well 2012
27" (69 cm) tall by 17" (43 cm) wide
Woven on a 35" (88.9 cm)-wide peg loom made by Suzanne Coleman.

Out of the Mist 2013
29½" (75 cm) tall by 8" (20 cm) wide
The arch and circle of the tapestry were woven on Dewberry Ridge ¼" (6 mm)-diameter weaving sticks. The face was woven on a Mirrix tapestry loom; the body, arms, and hood were woven on a Saori loom.

Sun Setting Moon Rising 2012–2013
14½" (36 cm) tall by 7" (17.5 cm) wide
The center panel was woven on a Mirrix tapestry loom. The outer frame was woven on a Dewberry Ridge 15" (37.5 cm)-wide peg loom with ¼" (6 mm)-diameter pegs.

Blythe Spirit 2013
10¼" (26 cm) tall by 6½" (16 cm) wide
The center panel was woven on a Mirrix tapestry loom. The outer frame was woven on a Dewberry Ridge 15" (37.5 cm)-wide peg loom with ¼" (6 mm)-diameter pegs.

Weaving Terms

Bloom. Sometimes the weaving will expand after the weaving is completed and the piece is off the loom. A good way to discover if the yarns are going to do this is to weave a swatch. (Don't like swatching? See SWATCH.)

Cartoon. A line drawing, template, or pattern for a tapestry.

Channel. Weaving on a peg loom or weaving stick creates ridges of weft strands that have warp strands running through them. These are referred to as "channels." Warp ends and weft ends are woven through them for finishing.

Cut length of warp strands. The cut length of the warp strands is the length of yarn that is cut to become the warp strands. It is twice as long as the working length of the warp yarn because the yarn must be folded in half at the hole in the peg after it is threaded into the peg or weaving stick.

Damascus edge. A strong method of finishing warp ends by tying them in double Damascus knots. See page 17 for instructions.

Draw in. Some yarns contract after the weaving is completed and the piece is off the loom. A good way to find out if the yarns are going to do this is to weave a swatch. (Don't like swatching? See SWATCH.)

Fell line. The edge of weaving that has just been woven.

Half hitch knot. A loop of yarn twisted around a peg or weaving stick. Half hitch knots are used to begin and end weaving. They are also used as elements on their own at times. See page 24 for instructions.

Pass. Weft woven from one edge to the other across the pegs. A pass is half of a row.

Peg loom. A weaving loom in which pegs are held in holes vertically. See chapter 1 for more explanation.

Row. Two passes make a complete row. The yarn ends at the same place it began by moving from left to right and back from right to left, or vice versa.

Sett. The number of pegs to an inch. The diameter of the pegs and the spacing of the holes they go in determine the sett. The sett for weaving sticks is closer than for peg looms, as weaving sticks are held together with no gaps between them.

Swatch. A swatch is a small piece of weaving you make to see exactly how many pegs will give you the correct dimensions with the sett of the loom you are weaving on, with the warp and weft yarns that you have chosen, and for tension, bloom, or draw in. Weaving small circles, squares, leaf shapes, or hearts are all great choices for swatching. You'll be able to see how all the variables come together and make changes before investing a lot of time in weaving something that might not work in the first attempt. It's much better to weave a little and discover a lot, and as a bonus, you'll end up with useful shapes for embellishing or for making jewelry or masks. Win/win. Trust me—swatching is important!

Template. A pattern that can be the full shape of the finished piece or a smaller guide to help you achieve one particular shape you want to weave.

Tension. How tightly the weft is pulled around the weaving sticks or pegs.

Warp. The strands that run lengthwise through the weaving providing the framework, or skeleton, for the weaving. The warp strands are completely covered by the weft strands. See chapter 2 for more information about choosing yarn for the warp for peg loom weaving.

Warping the loom. Cutting the strands of warp yarn and threading them through the holes in the pegs, then placing the pegs in the proper holes.

Weaving sticks. Sticks that are pointed on one end and have a hole through the other that can be held in the hand for weaving. See page 3 for further explanation.

Weft. The strands that are woven in and out through the pegs, covering the warp strands completely.

Working length of warp yarn. The length of the warp yarn that is calculated by adding several inches to each end of the desired length of the finished project. It is half the length of the cut length of the warp yarn, as the warp strands go through the hole in the peg and the ends are pulled out even so the center of the yarn is at the hole, doubling the warp strands at the center.

WPI (wraps per inch). The number of times the yarn wraps around 1" (2.5 cm) on a ruler. This information is essential when you want to substitute a different yarn from the one suggested in the pattern.

Yarn. See chapter 2 for more information about choosing yarn for peg loom weaving. Peg looms work wonderfully well with almost anything that can be bent easily. You can use purchased yarn, hand-spun yarn, locks of wool or other animal fibers, T-shirt yarn, ribbon, cord, string, twine, cassette tape, roving, or fabric strips (torn or cut).

Resources

Online, Internet, Social Media

Facebook group: facebook.com/groups/PegLooms/

A very active, friendly group with lots of photos, advice freely given, and abundant enthusiasm.

Ravelry group: ravelry.com/groups/pegs—sticks

This is a wonderful, friendly, and active group. Lots of information and inspiration! It's moderated by the lovely Suzanne Coleman, who also makes weaving sticks and peg looms: weavingmehome.com and/or etsy.com/uk/shop/WeavingMeHome.

My blog: tottietalkscrafts.com/

Search for "Peg Loom Weaving" to go directly to posts about peg looms and stick weaving and for "Woven Women" to see tapestries I have woven on peg looms.

My YouTube how-to videos: youtube.com/user/NoreenCroneFindlay

My Etsy shop: NCroneFindlay.etsy.com

Patterns and eBooks for designs that are not in this book.

My Facebook page: facebook.com/NoreenCroneFindlayDesigns

My Pinterest page: pinterest.com/cronefindlay/

I'll start a couple of Pinterest group pages for photos of things that you have woven from this book. I would love to see you post them on Pinterest.

My friend Caroline Halfyard designs the most delightful things with weaving sticks. You can see her work on her Pinterest page: pinterest.com/Yarnnannie/things-ive-made/

Sources and Suppliers

Peg Looms and Weaving Sticks

Dewberry Ridge, dewberryridge.com (wooden weaving sticks and peg looms)

Daisy Hill Handiworks, daisyhillhandiworks.blogspot.com and facebook.com/daisyhillhandiworks (nylon weaving sticks and peg looms)

Daegrad Tools, etsy.com/ca/shop/Daegrad and stores.ebay.co.uk/daegrad (steel weaving sticks)

Lacis Museum of Lace and Textiles, lacis.com (stick loom with aluminum needles)

Suzanne Coleman, weavingmehome.com and/or etsy.com/uk/shop/WeavingMeHome (peg looms)

Yarn

There are many, many yarn and fabric sources. Those listed here contributed materials for this book.

Briggs & Little, briggsandlittle.com (wool yarn and roving)

Lion Brand, lionbrand.com (acrylic and other yarn)

Nomad Fibreworks, nomadfibreworks.com/ (hand-spun yarn)